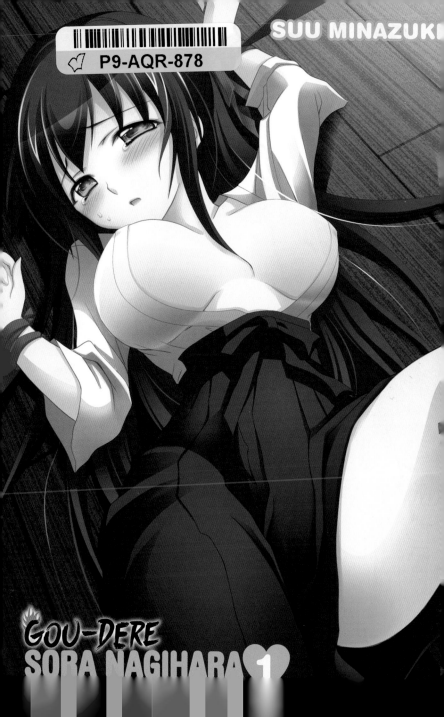

SUU MINAZUKI

GOU-DERE
SORA NAGIHARA ♥1♥

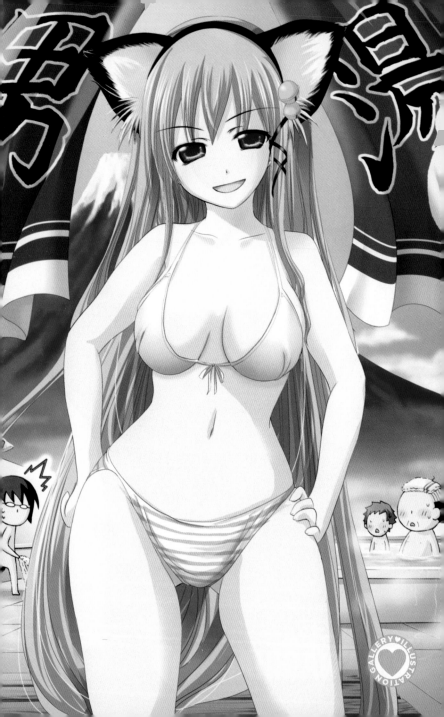

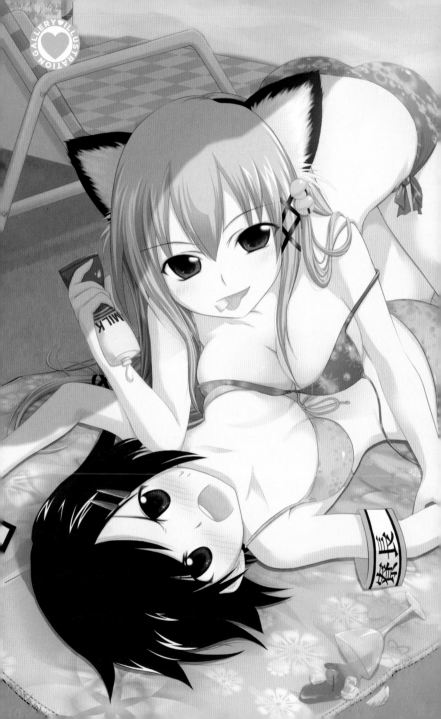

MY NAME IS SHOUTA YAMAKAWA, AND I'M A FIRST-YEAR IN HIGH SCHOOL.

...I LOVE THE WORLD OF 2-D.

I KNOW THIS IS KINDA SUDDEN SINCE WE'VE ONLY JUST MET AND ALL, BUT...

I'M...

...TO HAVE MET YOU.

I'M SO GLAD

AND MY TEST RESULTS SHOW...

I ONLY HAVE A LITTLE TIME LEFT...

CHAPTER 15

ABLE EMOTIONS

YOU COULD EVEN SAY I'M DOWNRIGHT PROUD OF IT.

IN SHORT, I'M HEAD OVER HEELS FOR ALL THINGS 2-D.

OHH...

I LOVE ALL THE BRIGHT COLORS.

THE JEWEL-LIKE EYES.

...BY MY SIDE...

I'M SO FLAT...

DON'T...

IF ONLY I HAD A GIRL LIKE HER...

THAT WOULD BE SORA NAGIHARA FROM TAMA × KISS.

...SHE IS A WONDER.

AND I, SHOUTA, HAVE OF LATE FALLEN IN LOVE—WITH SOMEONE 2-D, OF COURSE.

I'M SO GL...

...TO HAVE MET YOU.

CHAPTER 15 UNCONCEIVABLE EMO YOO SEO

HUH...?

KA GLASHO

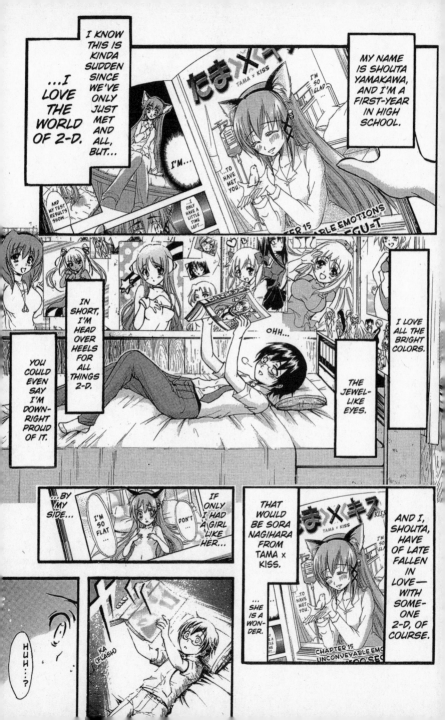

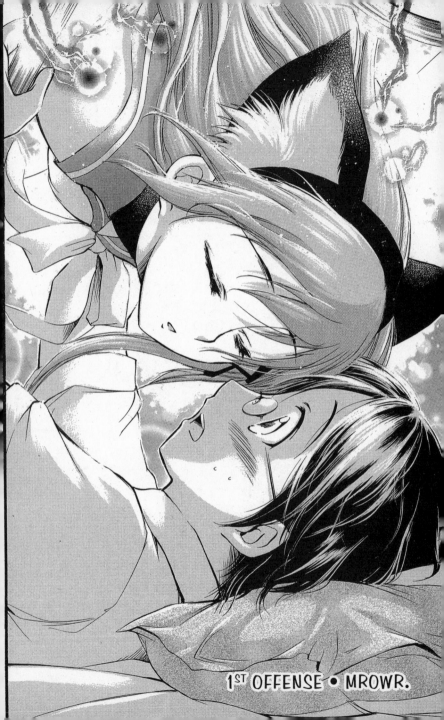

1ST OFFENSE • MROWR.

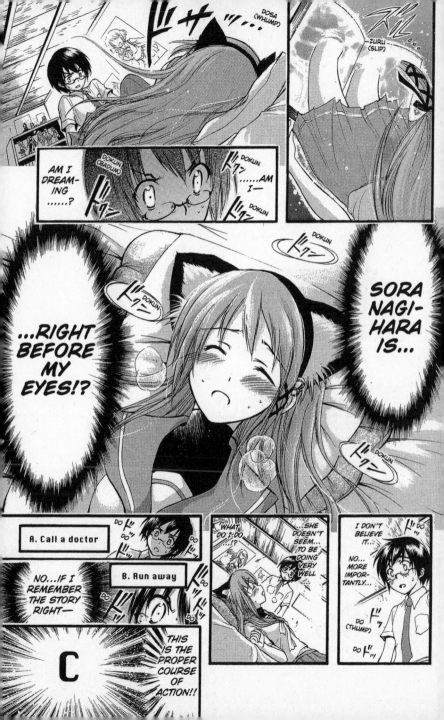

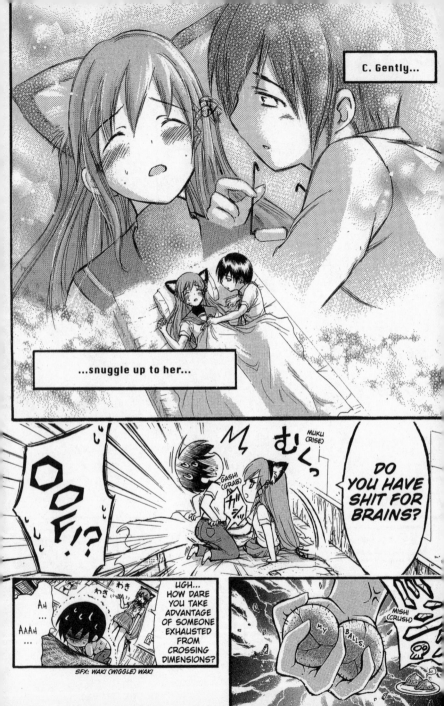

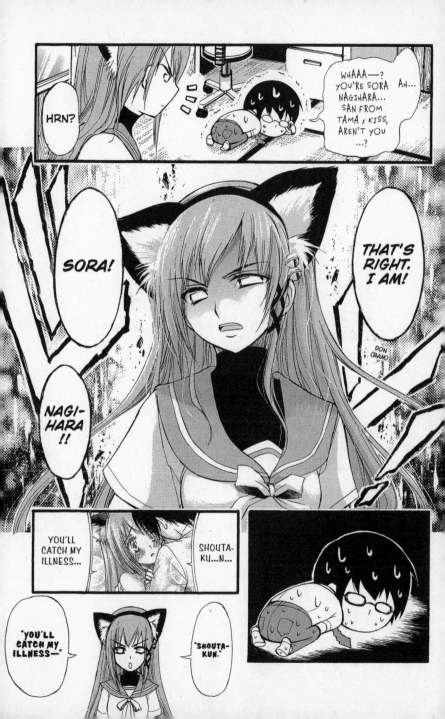

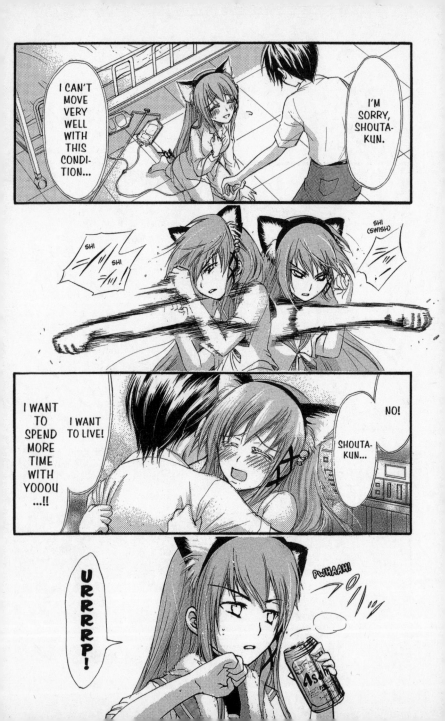

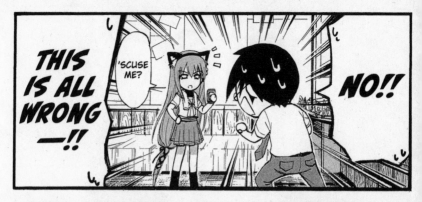

THIS IS ALL WRONG—!!

'SCUSE ME?

NO!!

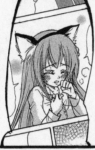

SHE'S AN ADMIRABLE GIRL WHO WEARS CAT EARS IN THE HOPE THAT SHE'LL COME BACK IN HER NEXT LIFE AS SOMEONE WITH THE FREEDOM OF A CAT TO EXPLORE THE WORLD OUTSIDE...

BORN WITH A FATAL DISEASE, SORA CAN'T SET FOOT OUTSIDE HER HOSPITAL ROOM...

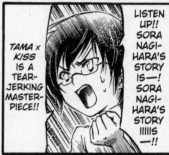

TAMA × KISS IS A TEARJERKING MASTERPIECE!!

LISTEN UP!! SORA NAGIHARA'S STORY IS—! SORA NAGIHARA'S STORY IIIIIS—!!

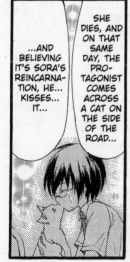

...AND BELIEVING IT'S SORA'S REINCARNATION, HE... KISSES... IT...

SHE DIES, AND ON THAT SAME DAY, THE PROTAGONIST COMES ACROSS A CAT ON THE SIDE OF THE ROAD...

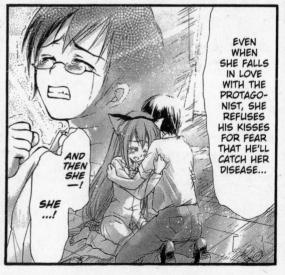

AND THEN SHE—!

SHE...!

EVEN WHEN SHE FALLS IN LOVE WITH THE PROTAGONIST, SHE REFUSES HIS KISSES FOR FEAR THAT HE'LL CATCH HER DISEASE...

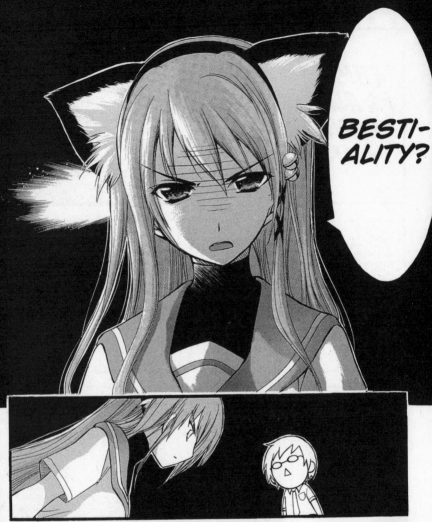

BESTI-
ALITY?

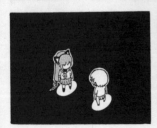
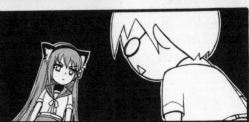

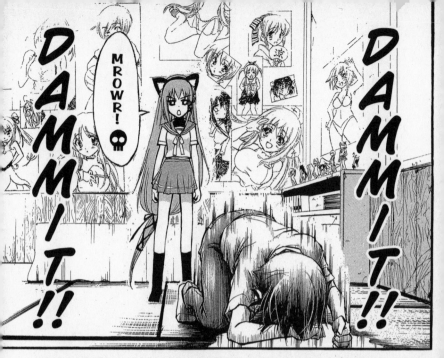

DAMMIT!!

MROWR! 💀

DAMMIT!!

RETURN TO THE LAND OF 2-D BEFORE YOU DEFILE SORA'S IMAGE ANY FURTHER!! I'M BEGGING YOU!!

HRN?

...PLEASE, JUST GO HOME...

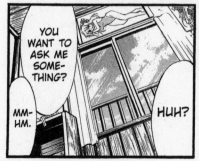

YOU WANT TO ASK ME SOMETHING?

MM-HM.

HUH?

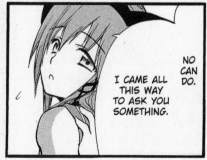

NO CAN DO.

I CAME ALL THIS WAY TO ASK YOU SOMETHING.

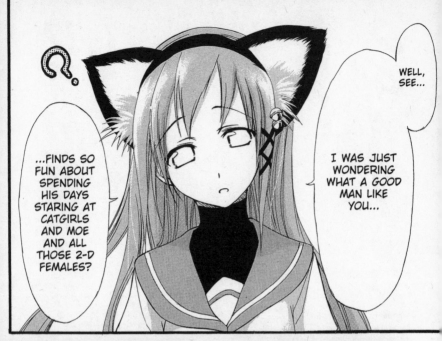

WELL, SEE...

I WAS JUST WONDERING WHAT A GOOD MAN LIKE YOU...

...FINDS SO FUN ABOUT SPENDING HIS DAYS STARING AT CATGIRLS AND MOE AND ALL THOSE 2-D FEMALES?

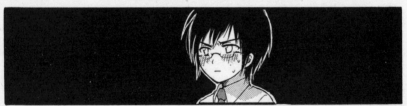

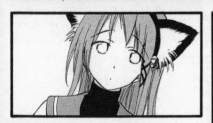

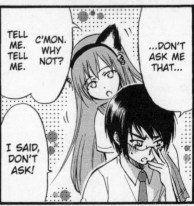

TELL ME. TELL ME.

C'MON. WHY NOT?

...DON'T ASK ME THAT...

I SAID, DON'T ASK!

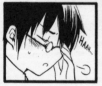

HAAH..

14

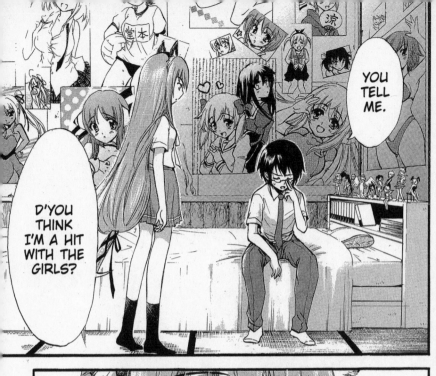

YOU TELL ME.

D'YOU THINK I'M A HIT WITH THE GIRLS?

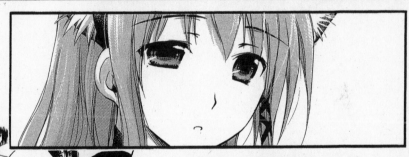

THEY LIKE ME REGARDLESS OF WHAT I'M LIKE—

AND, UM—

TO ME, 2-D GIRLS ARE MY "IDEAL."

WELL, THAT MIGHT JUST BE MY JEALOUSY TALKING.

BUT THERE ARE SOME THINGS YOU JUST CAN'T CHANGE.

FOR ALL THE GUYS BORN WITH NATURAL ATHLETICISM OR GOOD LOOKS, THERE ARE SHRIMPS IN GLASSES LIKE ME.

LIFE'S NOT FAIR.

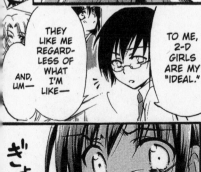

ぎょっ
GYO
(SHOCK)

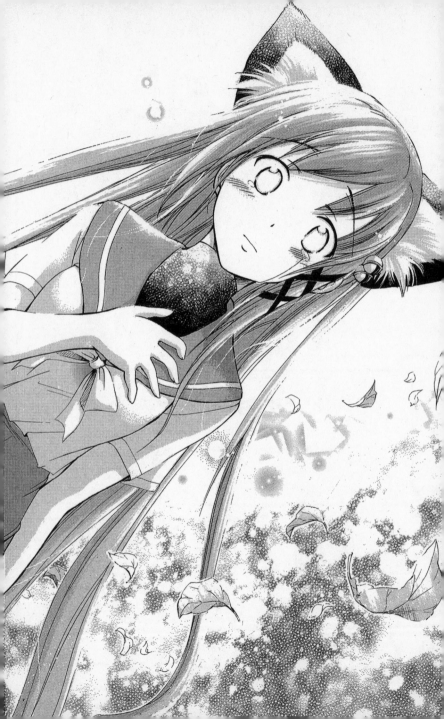

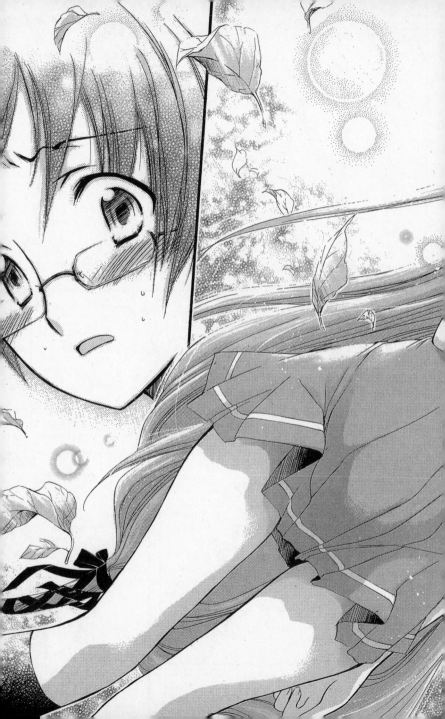

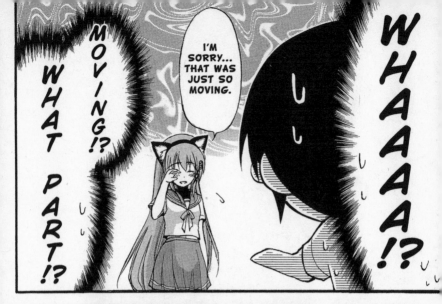

MOVING!? WHAT PART!?

I'M SORRY... THAT WAS JUST SO MOVING.

WHAAAAA!?

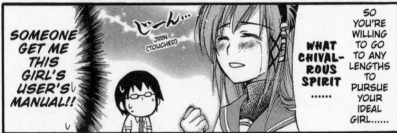

SOMEONE GET ME THIS GIRL'S USER'S MANUAL!!

じーん...
JIIIN (TOUCHED)

WHAT CHIVAL-ROUS SPIRIT ......

SO YOU'RE WILLING TO GO TO ANY LENGTHS TO PURSUE YOUR IDEAL GIRL......

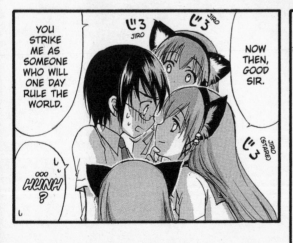

YOU STRIKE ME AS SOMEONE WHO WILL ONE DAY RULE THE WORLD.

...HUNH?

い3 JIRO
い3 JIRO
い3 JIRO (STARE)

NOW THEN, GOOD SIR.

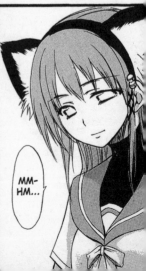

MM-HM...

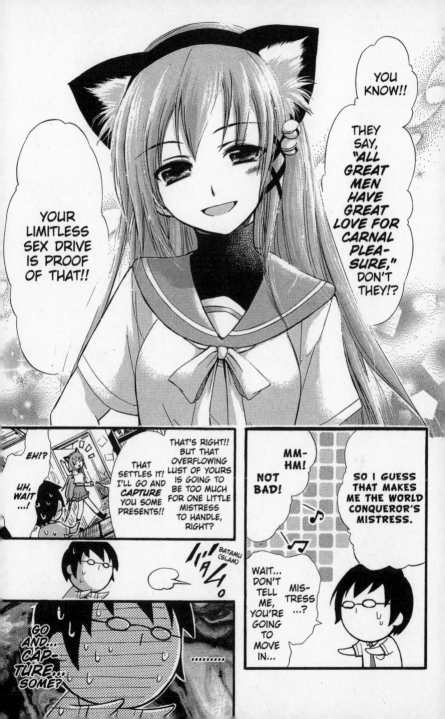

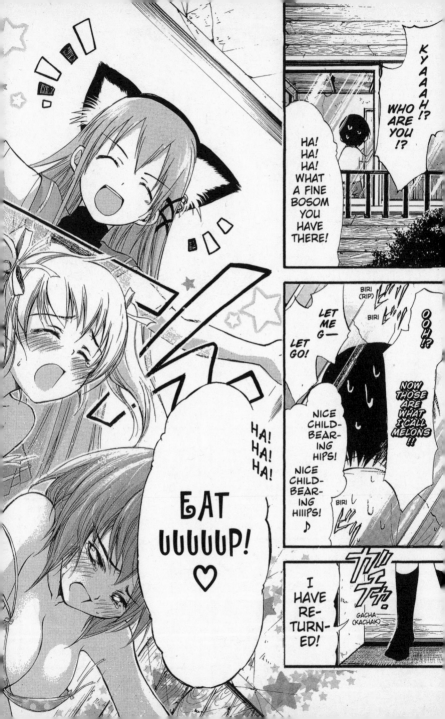

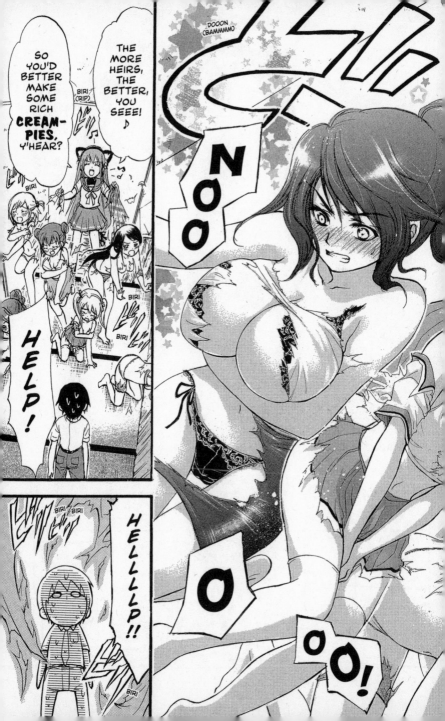

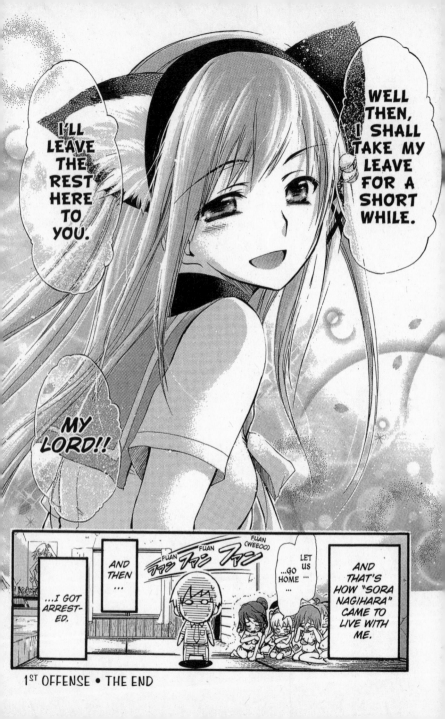

1ST OFFENSE • THE END

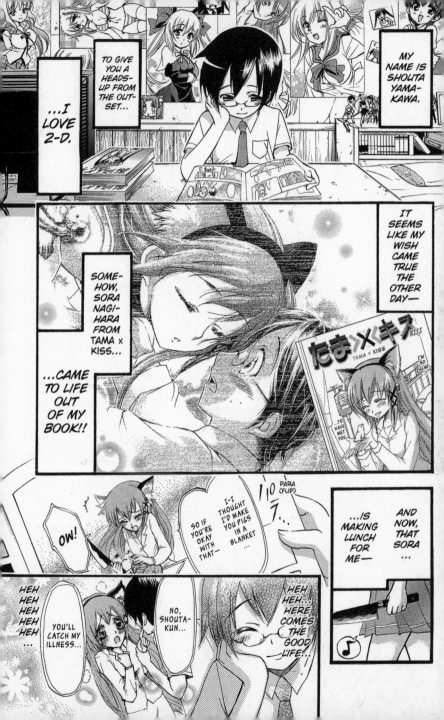

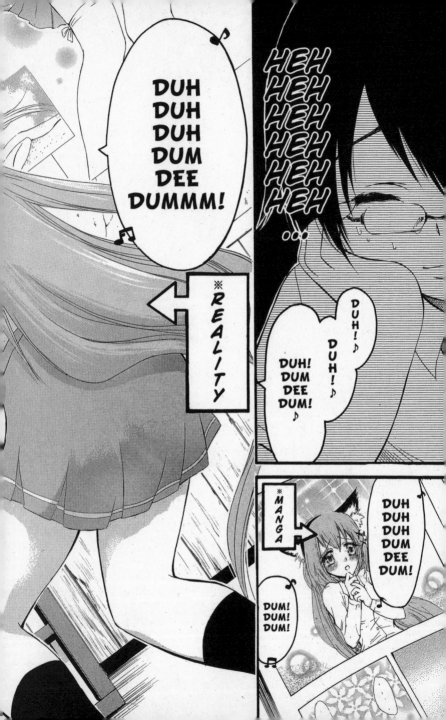

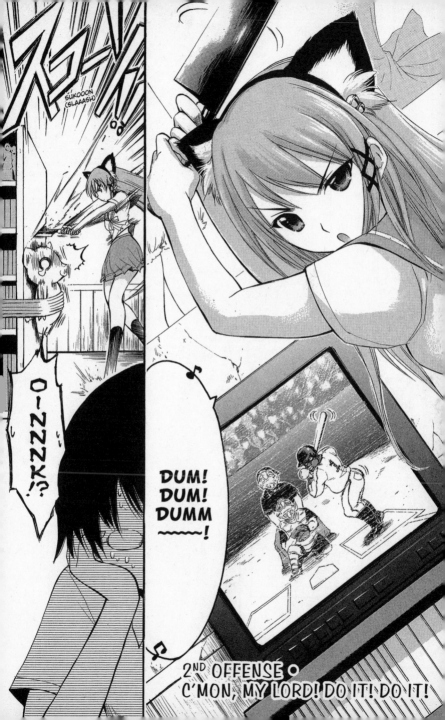

2ND OFFENSE ◦
C'MON, MY LORD! DO IT! DO IT!

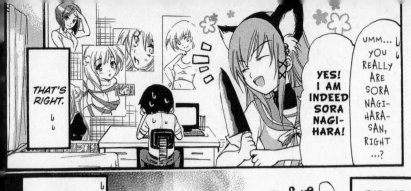

UMM... YOU REALLY ARE SORA NAGIHARA-SAN, RIGHT ...?

YES! I AM INDEED SORA NAGIHARA!

THAT'S RIGHT.

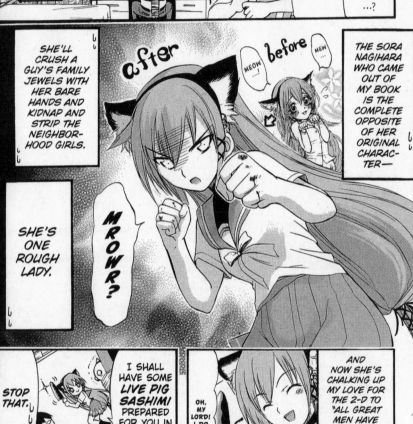

THE SORA NAGIHARA WHO CAME OUT OF MY BOOK IS THE COMPLETE OPPOSITE OF HER ORIGINAL CHARACTER—

MEW ...

before

MEOW ...!

after

SHE'LL CRUSH A GUY'S FAMILY JEWELS WITH HER BARE HANDS AND KIDNAP AND STRIP THE NEIGHBORHOOD GIRLS.

MROWR?

SHE'S ONE ROUGH LADY.

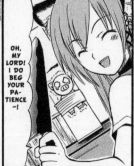

AND NOW SHE'S CHALKING UP MY LOVE FOR THE 2-D TO "ALL GREAT MEN HAVE GREAT LOVE FOR CARNAL PLEASURES" AND TELLING ME THAT I'M "SOMEONE WHO WILL ONE DAY RULE THE WORLD"—

OH, MY LORD! I DO BEG YOUR PATIENCE ~!

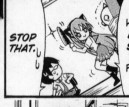

STOP THAT.

I SHALL HAVE SOME LIVE PIG SASHIMI PREPARED FOR YOU IN NO TIME.

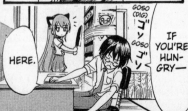

HERE.

IF YOU'RE HUNGRY—

GOSO (DIG)
ゴソゴソ

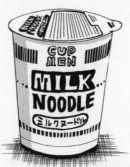

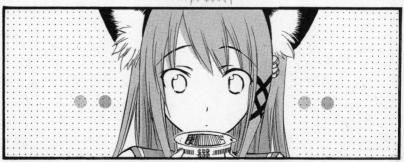

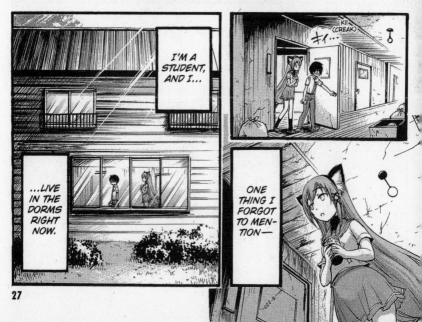

I'M A STUDENT, AND I...

...LIVE IN THE DORMS RIGHT NOW.

KII (CREAK)

ONE THING I FORGOT TO MEN-TION—

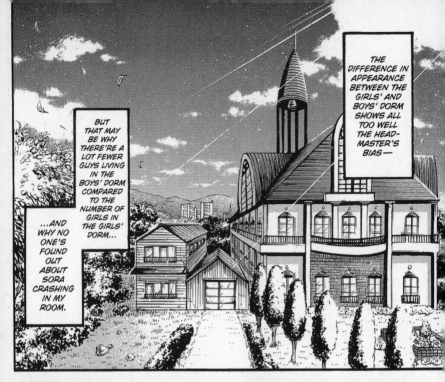

THE DIFFERENCE IN APPEARANCE BETWEEN THE GIRLS' AND BOYS' DORM SHOWS ALL TOO WELL THE HEAD-MASTER'S BIAS—

BUT THAT MAY BE WHY THERE'RE A LOT FEWER GUYS LIVING IN THE BOYS' DORM COMPARED TO THE NUMBER OF GIRLS IN THE GIRLS' DORM...

...AND WHY NO ONE'S FOUND OUT ABOUT SORA CRASHING IN MY ROOM.

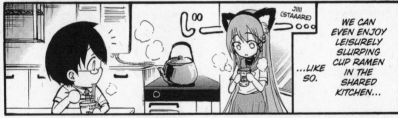

JIIII (STAAARE)

...LIKE SO.

WE CAN EVEN ENJOY LEISURELY SLURPING CUP RAMEN IN THE SHARED KITCHEN...

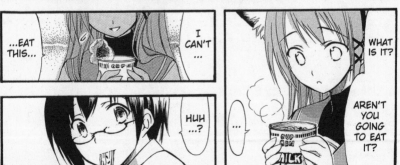

...EAT THIS...

I CAN'T...

HUH...?

...

WHAT IS IT?

AREN'T YOU GOING TO EAT IT?

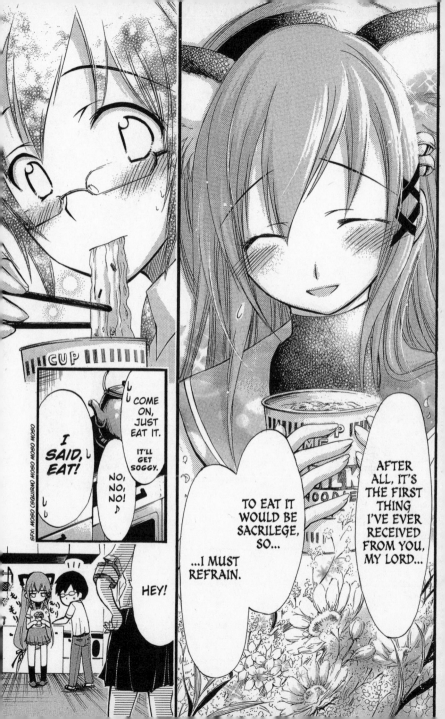

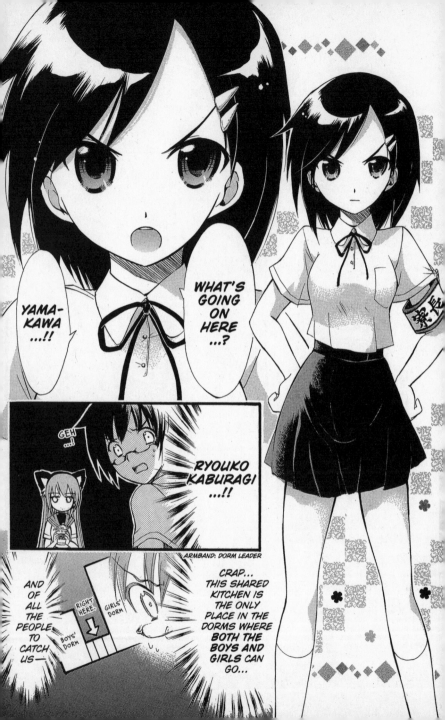

YAMA-KAWA...!!

WHAT'S GOING ON HERE...?

GEH...!

RYOUKO KABURAGI...!!

ARMBAND: DORM LEADER

AND OF ALL THE PEOPLE TO CATCH US—

RIGHT HERE.

BOYS' DORM

GIRLS' DORM

CRAP... THIS SHARED KITCHEN IS THE ONLY PLACE IN THE DORMS WHERE BOTH THE BOYS AND GIRLS CAN GO...

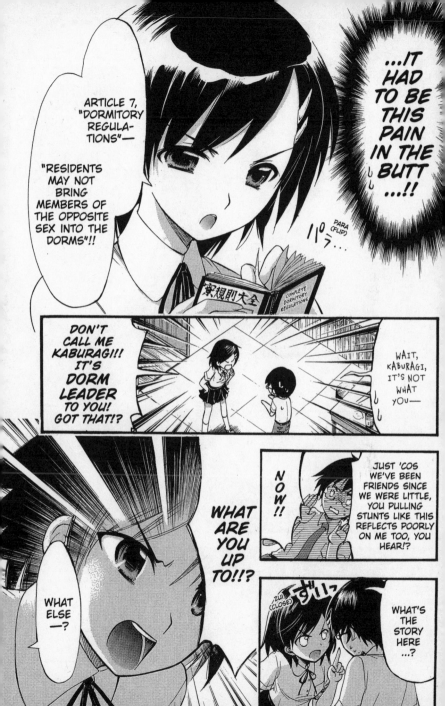

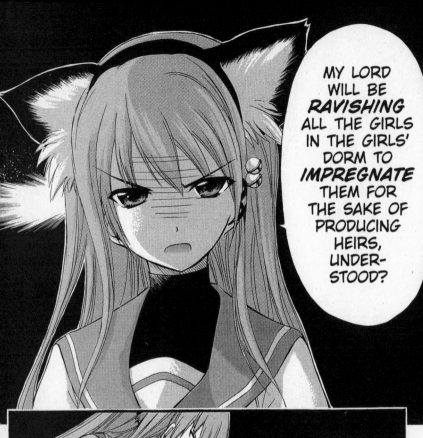

MY LORD WILL BE **RAVISHING** ALL THE GIRLS IN THE GIRLS' DORM TO **IMPREGNATE** THEM FOR THE SAKE OF PRODUCING HEIRS, UNDERSTOOD?

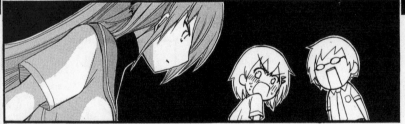

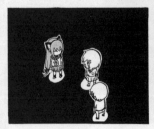

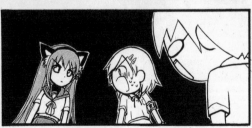

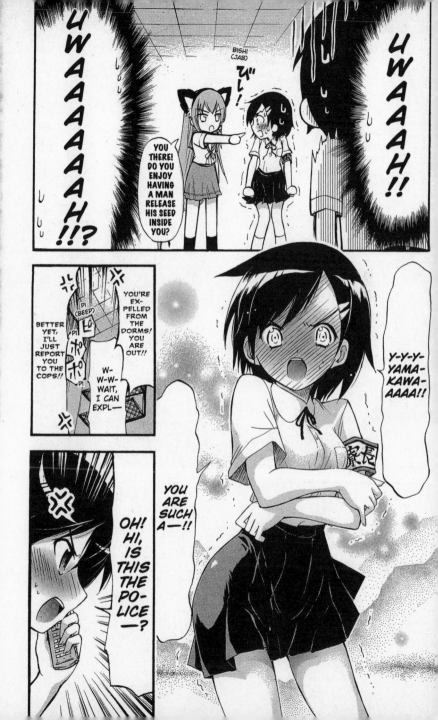

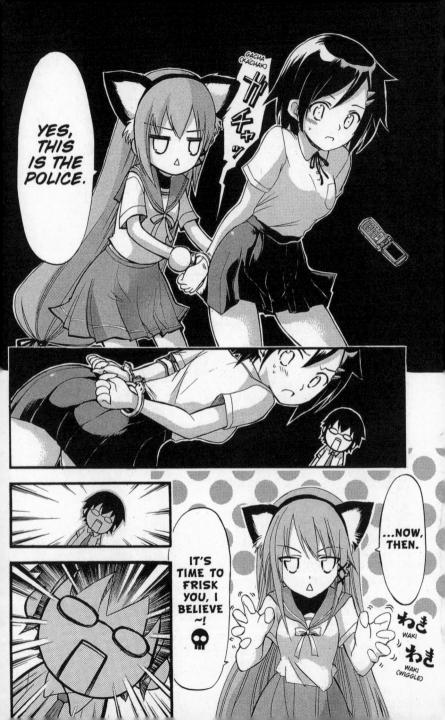

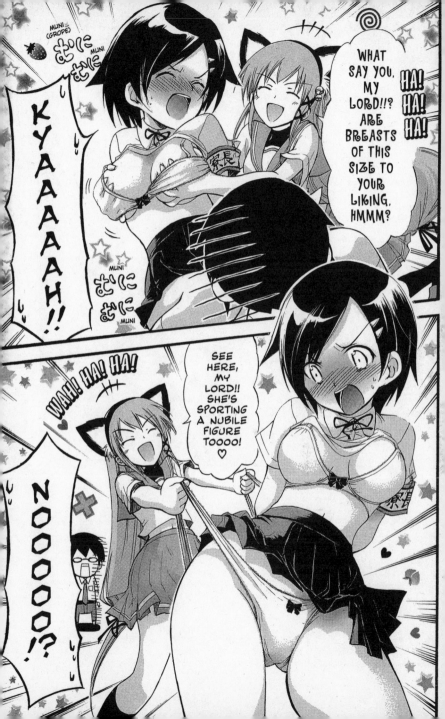

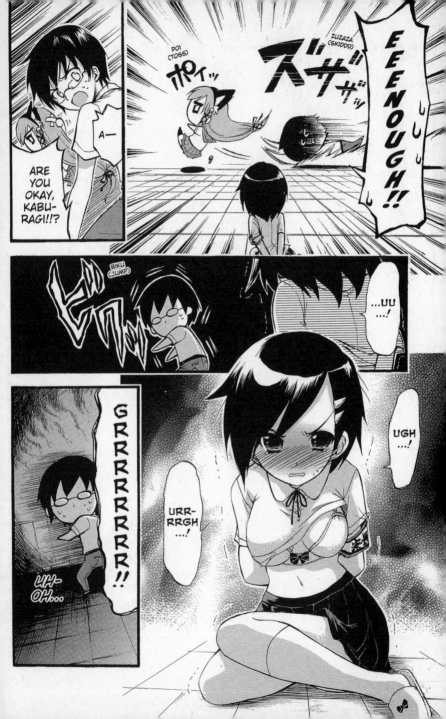

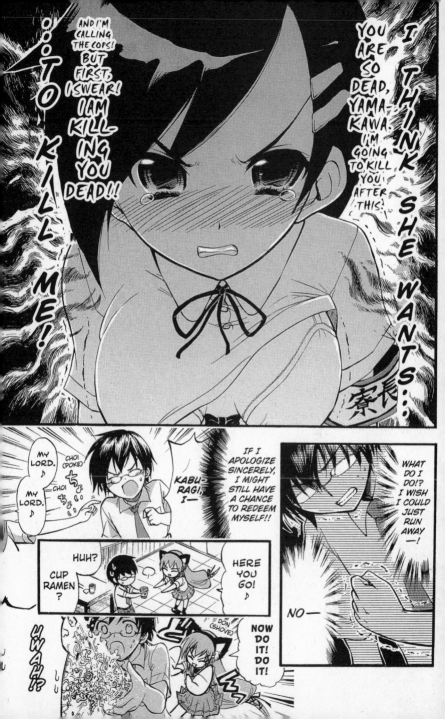

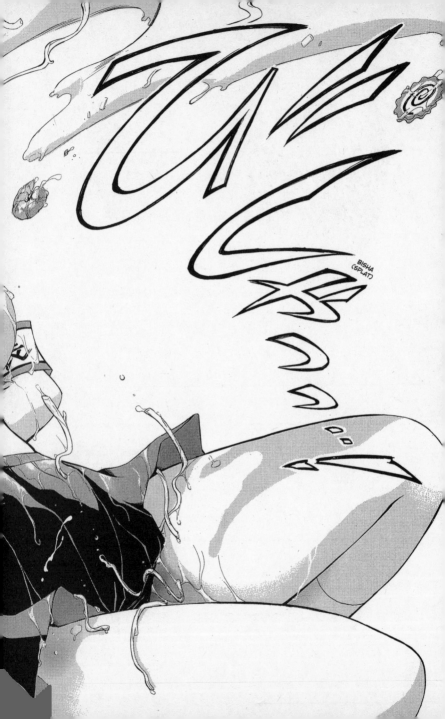

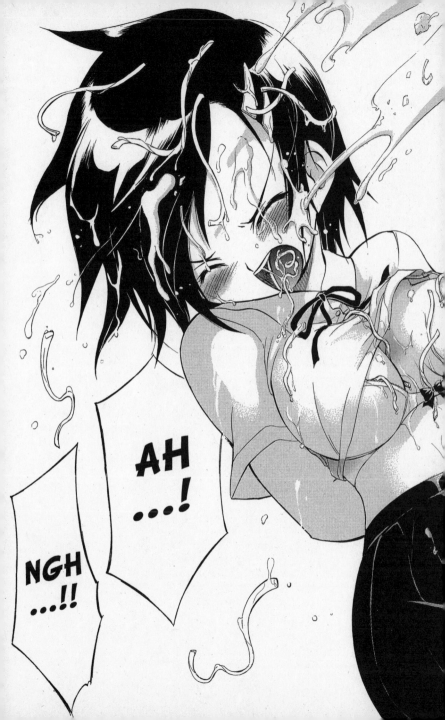

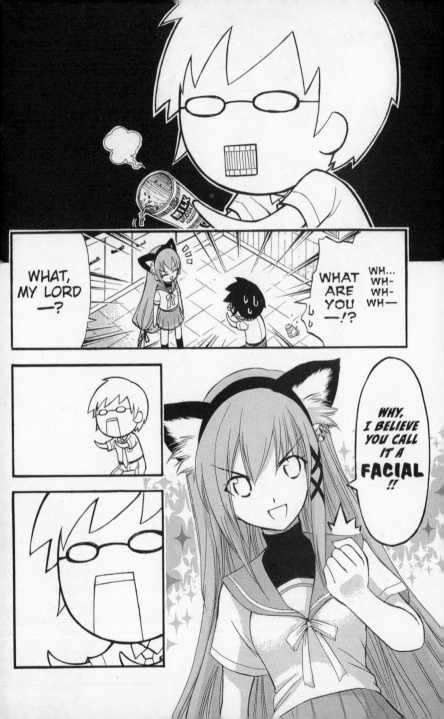

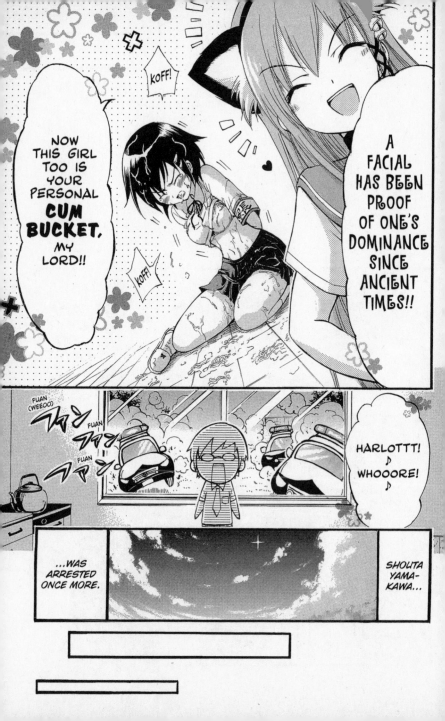

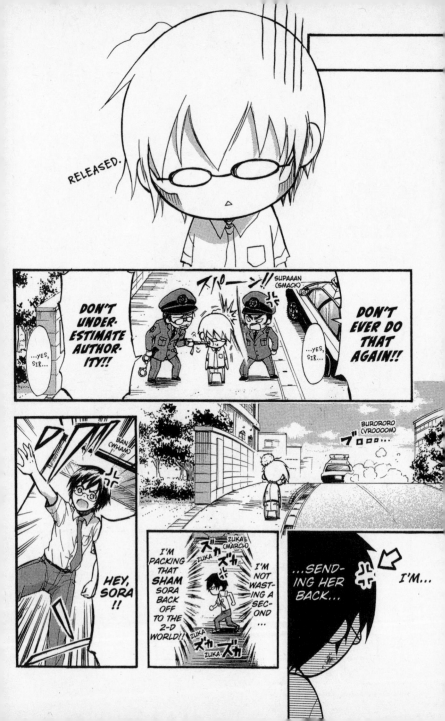

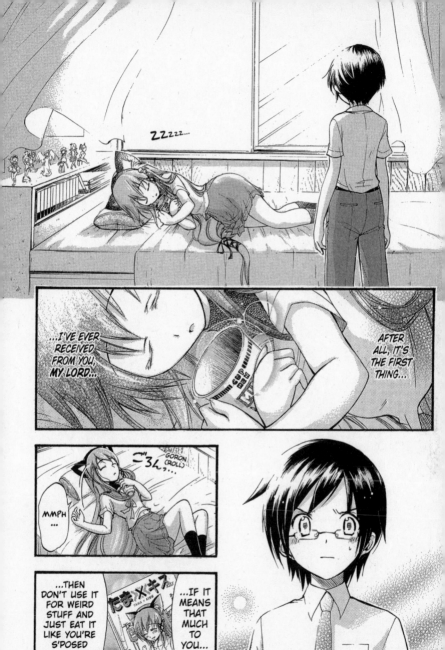

ZZzzz...

...I'VE EVER RECEIVED FROM YOU, MY LORD...

AFTER ALL, IT'S THE FIRST THING...

ごろん?... GORON (ROLL)

MMPH...

...THEN DON'T USE IT FOR WEIRD STUFF AND JUST EAT IT LIKE YOU'RE S'POSED TO...

...IF IT MEANS THAT MUCH TO YOU...

43

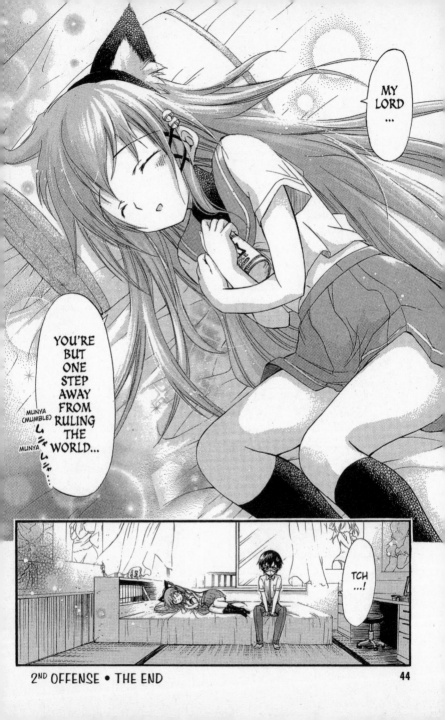

2ND OFFENSE • THE END

44

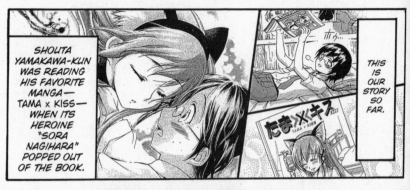

THIS IS OUR STORY SO FAR.

SHOLTA YAMAKAWA-KUN WAS READING HIS FAVORITE MANGA— TAMA × KISS— WHEN ITS HEROINE "SORA NAGIHARA" POPPED OUT OF THE BOOK.

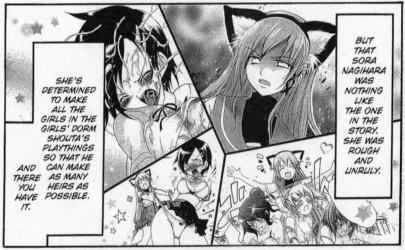

BUT THAT SORA NAGIHARA WAS NOTHING LIKE THE ONE IN THE STORY. SHE WAS ROUGH AND UNRULY.

SHE'S DETERMINED TO MAKE ALL THE GIRLS IN THE GIRLS' DORM SHOLTA'S PLAYTHINGS SO THAT HE CAN MAKE AS MANY HEIRS AS POSSIBLE.

AND THERE YOU HAVE IT.

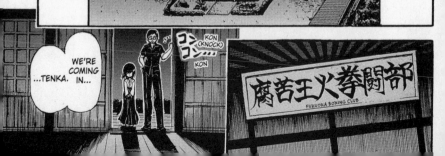

ANIMO PRIVATE ACADEMY

CLUB-ROOM WING—

...TENKA.

WE'RE COMING IN...

KON (KNOCK) KON

腐苦王火拳闘部
FUKUOKA BOXING CLUB

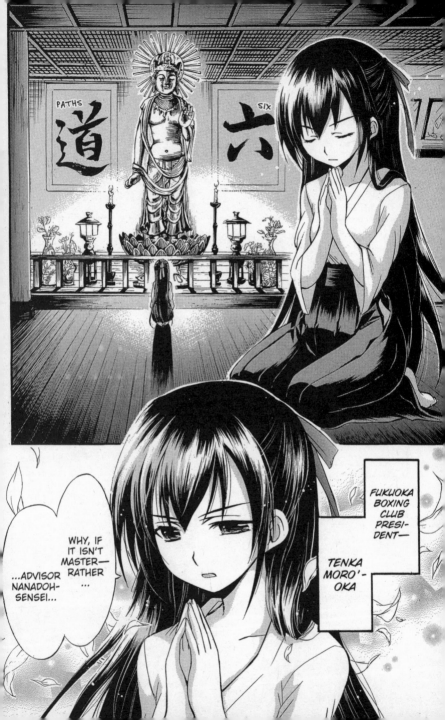

PATHS 道 六 SIX

WHY, IF IT ISN'T MASTER— RATHER ...

...ADVISOR NANADOH-SENSEI...

FUKUOKA BOXING CLUB PRESI-DENT—

TENKA MORO'-OKA

HEH-HEH... EVEN THOUGH YOU'VE SURPASSED ME, YOUR TEACHER...?

I STILL HAVE MUCH TO LEARN...

YOU'RE HERE SO LATE AT NIGHT... WHAT A HARD WORKER...

......

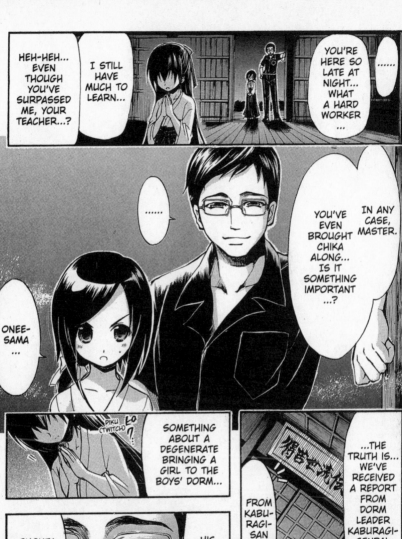

......

YOU'VE EVEN BROUGHT CHIKA ALONG... IS IT SOMETHING IMPORTANT...?

IN ANY CASE, MASTER.

ONEE-SAMA...

PIKU (TWITCH)

?

SOMETHING ABOUT A DEGENERATE BRINGING A GIRL TO THE BOYS' DORM...

FROM KABU-RAGI-SAN...?

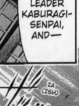

...THE TRUTH IS... WE'VE RECEIVED A REPORT FROM DORM LEADER KABURAGI-SENPAI, AND—

SHOUTA YAMAKAWA.

HIS NAME—

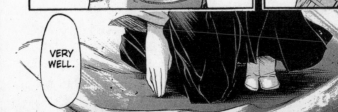

VERY WELL.

ZA (ZSH)

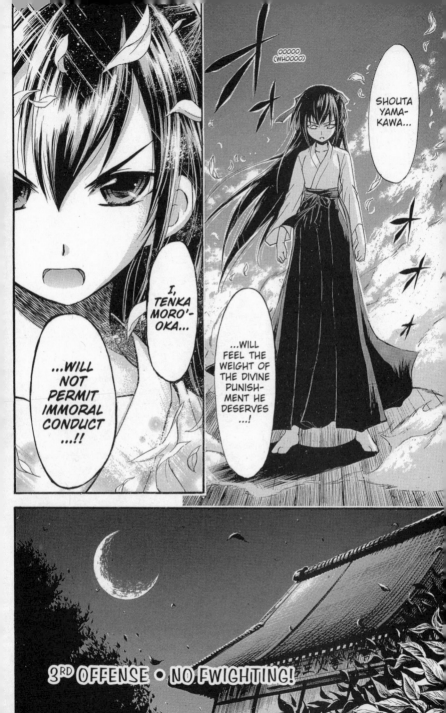

3RD OFFENSE • NO FWIGHTING!

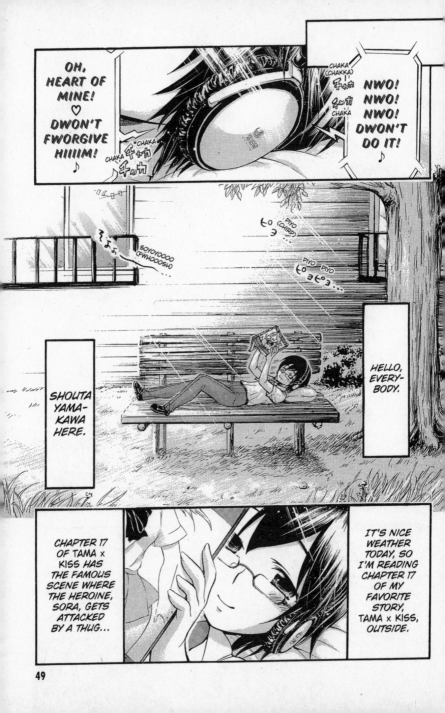

OH, HEART OF MINE! ♡ DWON'T FWORGIVE HIIIIM! ♪

CHAKA "CHAKA 千ャ々 千ャ々

CHAKA (CHAKKA) 千ャ々 千ャ々 CHAKA

NWO! NWO! NWO! DWON'T DO IT! ♪

PIYO (CHIRP) ♪

SOYOYOOO (FWHOOOSH)

PIYO PIYO

SHOUTA YAMAKAWA HERE.

HELLO, EVERYBODY.

CHAPTER 17 OF TAMA x KISS HAS THE FAMOUS SCENE WHERE THE HEROINE, SORA, GETS ATTACKED BY A THUG...

IT'S NICE WEATHER TODAY, SO I'M READING CHAPTER 17 OF MY FAVORITE STORY, TAMA x KISS, OUTSIDE.

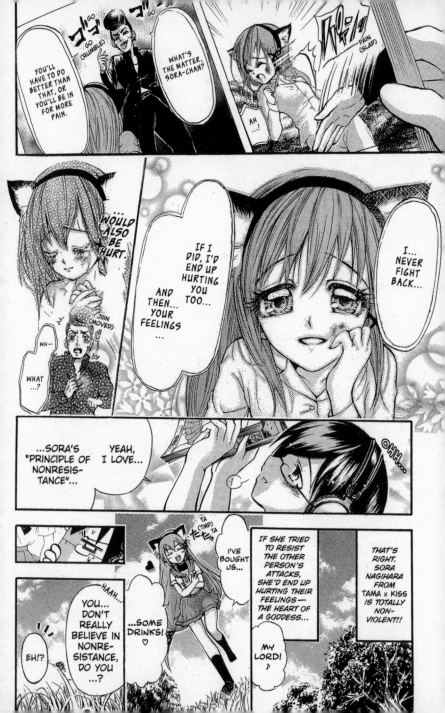

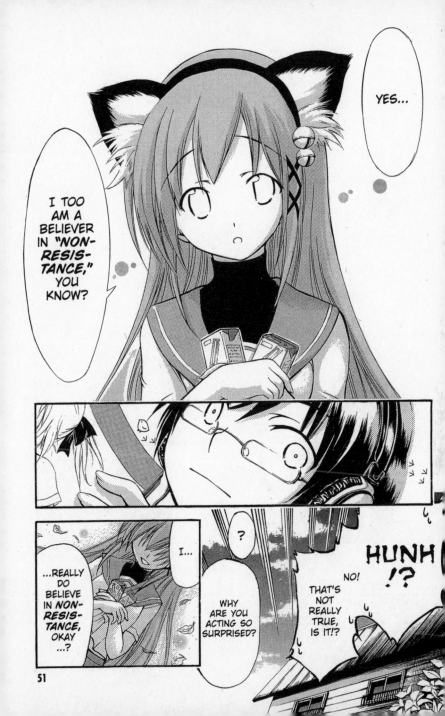

YES...

I TOO AM A BELIEVER IN "NON-RESIS-TANCE," YOU KNOW?

...REALLY DO BELIEVE IN NON-RESIS-TANCE, OKAY...?

I...

?

WHY ARE YOU ACTING SO SURPRISED?

HUNH!?

NO! THAT'S NOT REALLY TRUE, IS IT!?

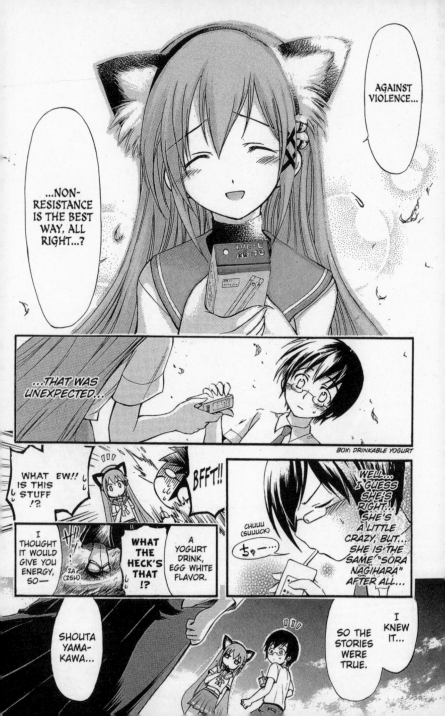

AGAINST VIOLENCE...

...NON-RESISTANCE IS THE BEST WAY, ALL RIGHT...?

...THAT WAS UNEXPECTED...

BOX: DRINKABLE YOGURT

WHAT IS THIS STUFF!?

EW!!

BFFT!!

I THOUGHT IT WOULD GIVE YOU ENERGY, SO—

ZA (ZSH)

WHAT THE HECK'S THAT!?

A YOGURT DRINK, EGG WHITE FLAVOR.

CHUUU (SUUUCK)

ちゅ—...

WELL... I GUESS SHE'S RIGHT... SHE'S A LITTLE CRAZY, BUT... SHE IS THE SAME "SORA NAGIHARA" AFTER ALL...

SHOUTA YAMA-KAWA...

SO THE STORIES WERE TRUE.

I KNEW IT...

AND I WILL NOT STAND FOR IT...!!

PRE-PARE YOUR-SELF!!

GEH...! THE FUKU-OKA BOXING CLUB!?

SO... WE'RE GETTING OUTTA HERE, SORA!!

YES.

OOOOOOO (WHOOO)

BRINGING A GIRL INTO THE BOYS' DORM...

...IS A MOST IMMORAL DEED...

ON DAYS OFF, THEY CHALLENGE OTHER DOJOS AND BRING THEM TO THEIR KNEES. THEY'RE A DANGEROUS BUNCH...!!

THEY'RE THE MOST POWERFUL MARTIAL ARTS CLUB ON CAMPUS—

FU-KUOKA BOXING?

OOOOOO

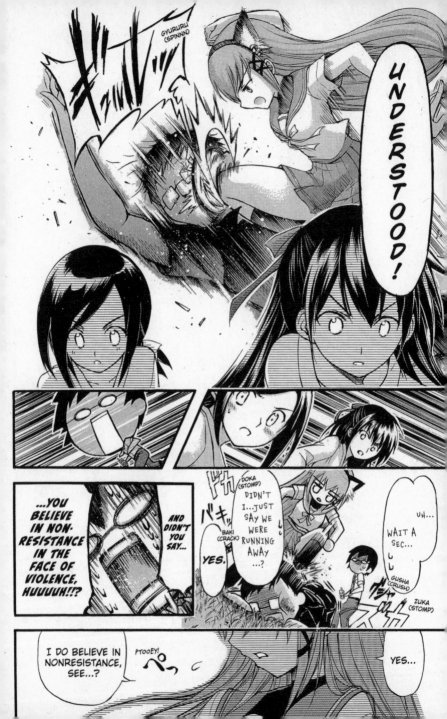

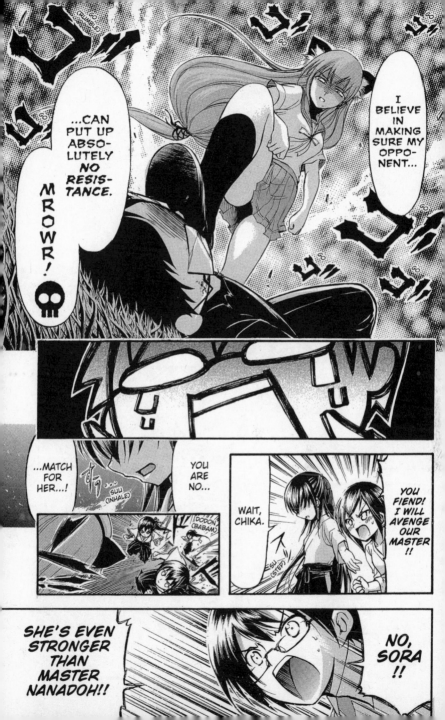

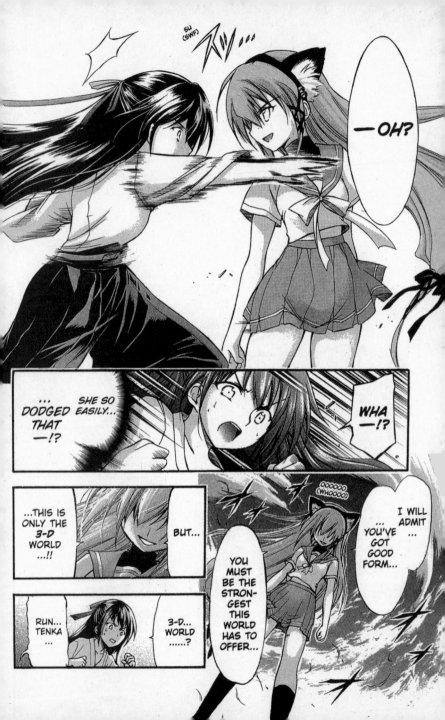

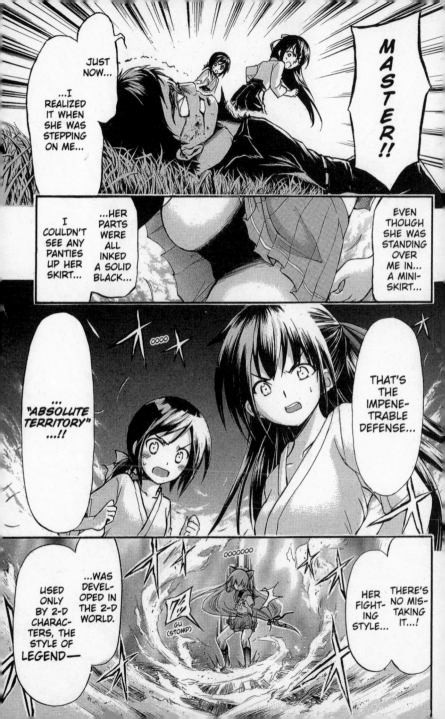

JUST NOW...

...I REALIZED IT WHEN SHE WAS STEPPING ON ME...

MASTER!!

I COULDN'T SEE ANY PANTIES UP HER SKIRT...

...HER PARTS WERE ALL INKED A SOLID BLACK...

EVEN THOUGH SHE WAS STANDING OVER ME IN... A MINI-SKIRT...

..."ABSOLUTE TERRITORY" ...!!

THAT'S THE IMPENE-TRABLE DEFENSE...

USED ONLY BY 2-D CHARAC-TERS, THE STYLE OF LEGEND—

...WAS DEVEL-OPED IN THE 2-D WORLD.

GU (STOMP)

HER FIGHT-ING STYLE...

THERE'S NO MIS-TAKING IT...!

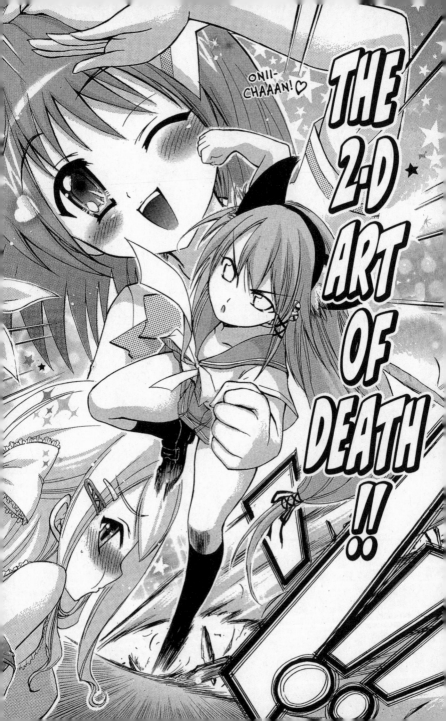

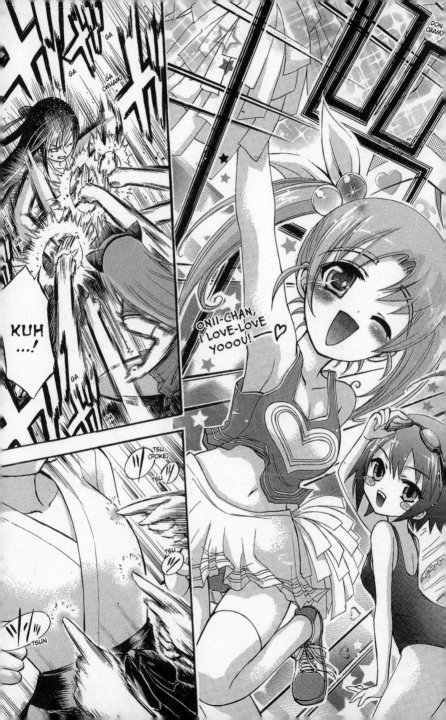

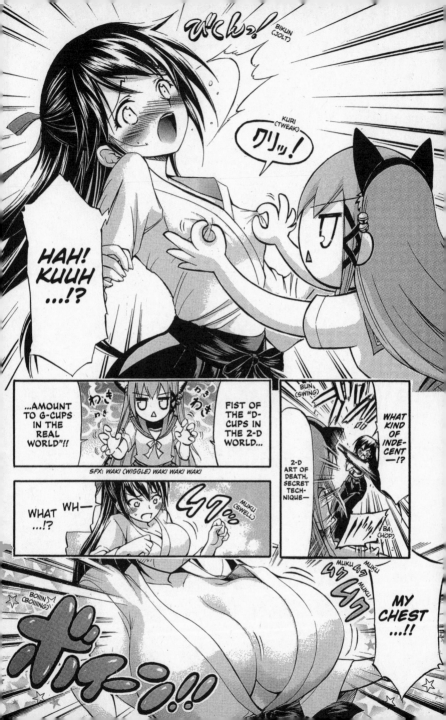

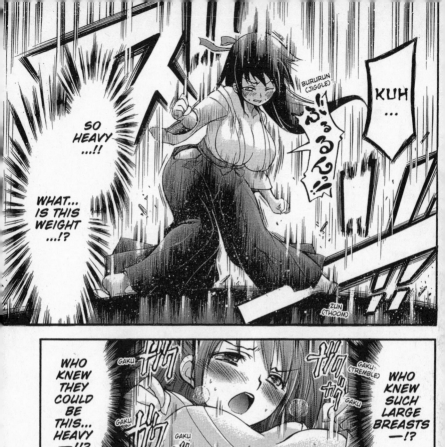

SO HEAVY ...!!

WHAT... IS THIS WEIGHT ...!?

BURURUN (JIGGLE)

KUH...

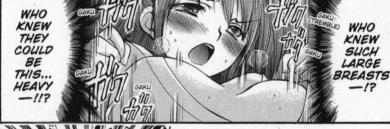

WHO KNEW THEY COULD BE THIS... HEAVY—!!?

GAKU

GAKU (TREMBLE)

GAKU

GAKU

WHO KNEW SUCH LARGE BREASTS—!!?

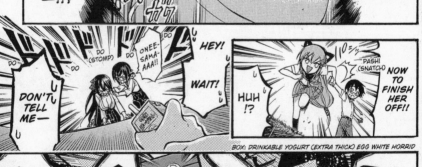

DO (STOMP)

DO

DO

DO

DO

ONEE-SAMA-AAA!!

HEY!

WAIT!

DON'T TELL ME—

HUH !?

PASHI (SNATCH)

NOW TO FINISH HER OFF!!

BOX: DRINKABLE YOGURT (EXTRA THICK) EGG WHITE HORRID

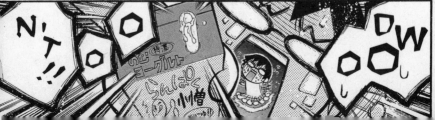

N'T!!

OW

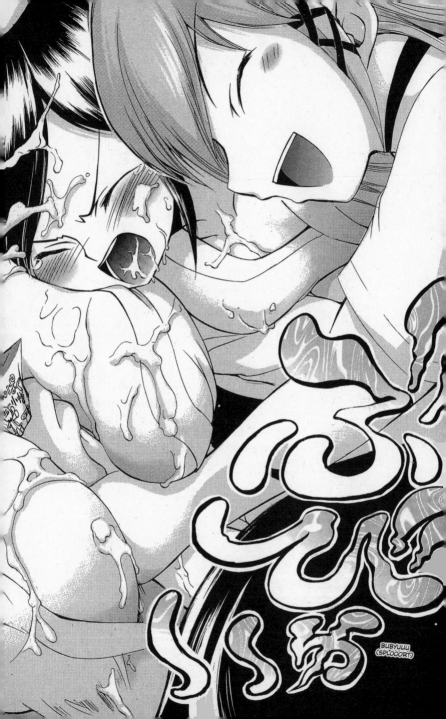

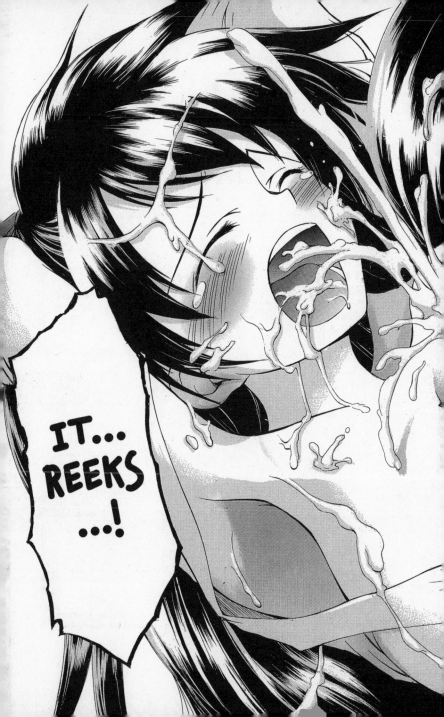

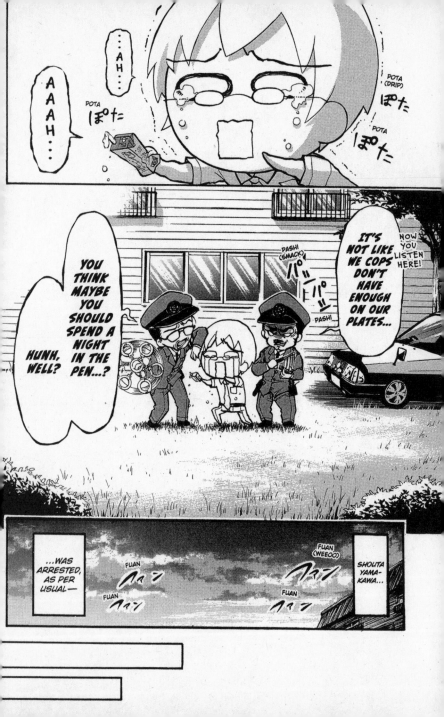

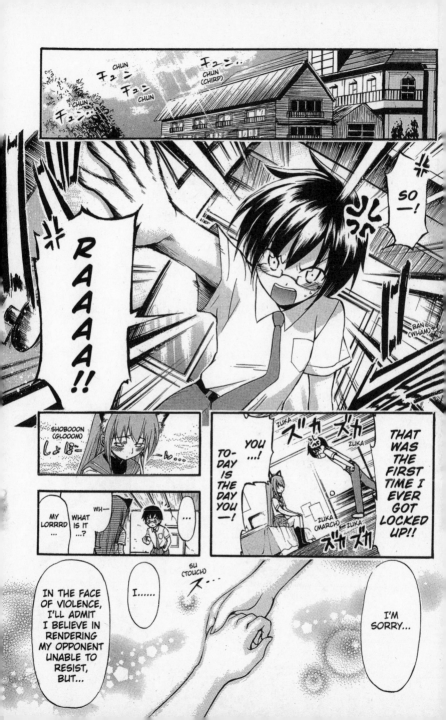

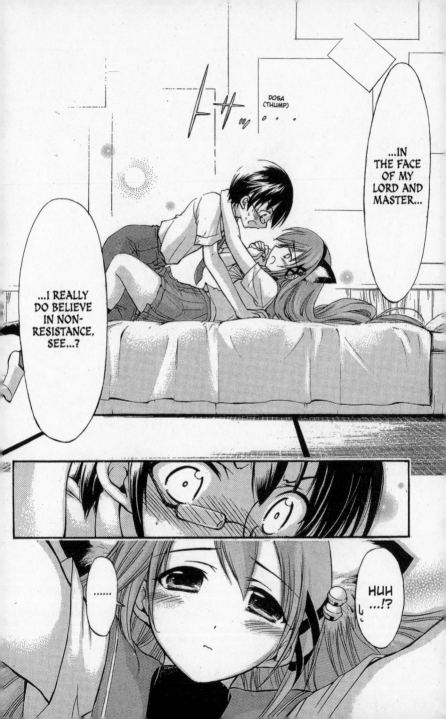

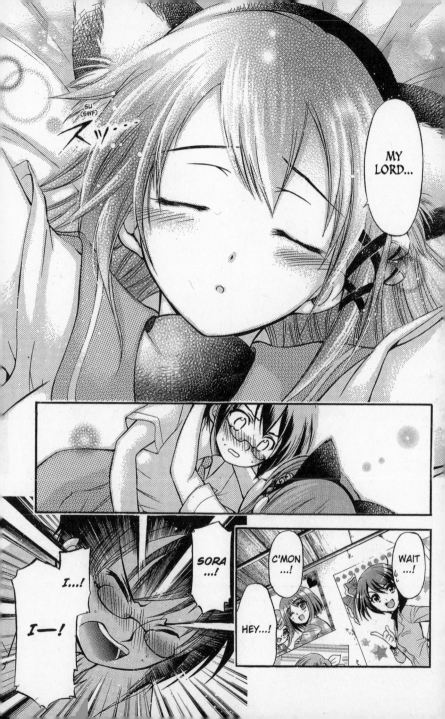

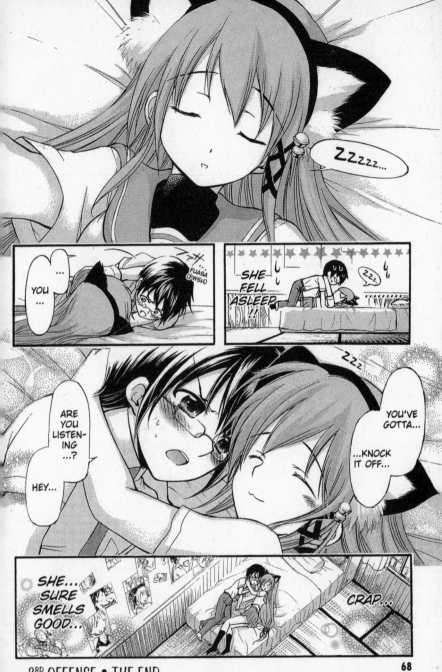

3RD OFFENSE • THE END

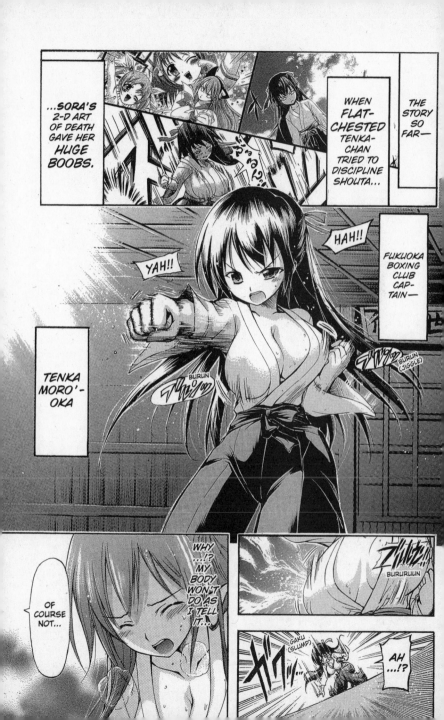

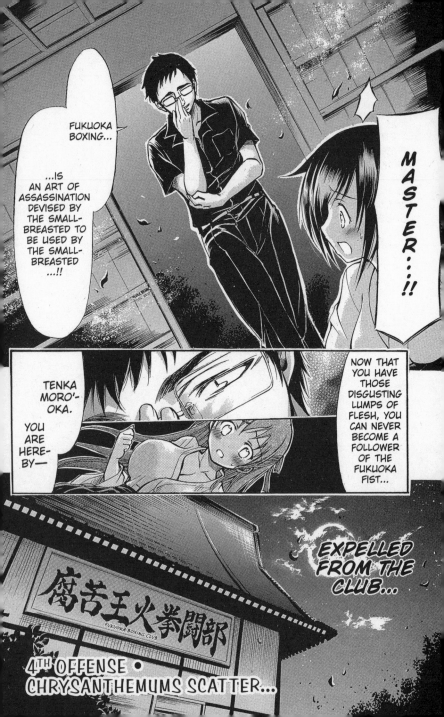

CHUN
(CHIRP)
チュン

CHUN CHUN
チュン チュン
CHUN
チュン

HUNH?

YOU WANT ME TO MAKE YOUR CHEST SMALL AGAIN?

...IT'S NO SMALL MATTER TO GO SHRINKING THEM WITHOUT HIS LEAVE—

WHA—!?

KAA (BLUSH)

...AS YOU NOW BELONG TO MY LORD...

YOUR REQUEST IS NOT IMPOSSIBLE, BUT...

HMPH...

THEN YOU'LL JUST HAVE TO ASK MY LORD YOURSELF...

AND DON'T MOST MEN PREFER BIG BOSOMS?

MOST GIRLS WOULD BE OVERJOYED AT HAVING SUCH GRAND BREASTS—

YOU REALLY ARE AN ODD ONE.

....

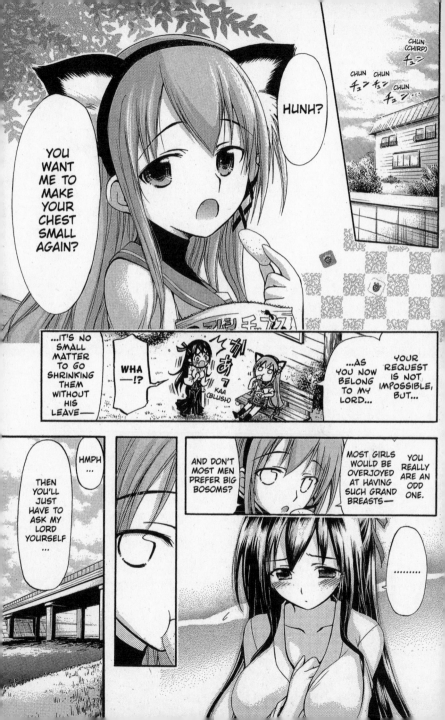

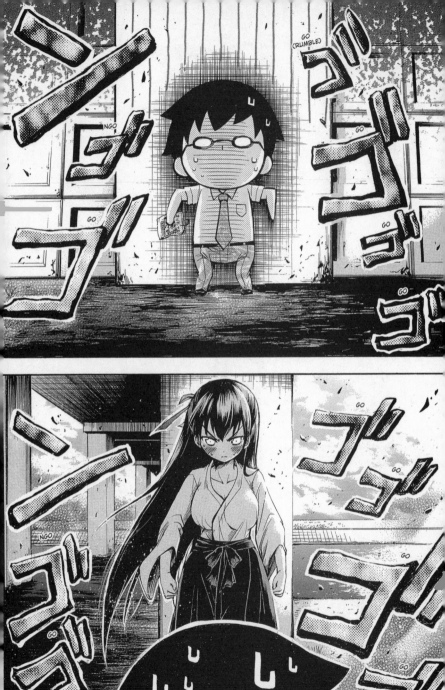

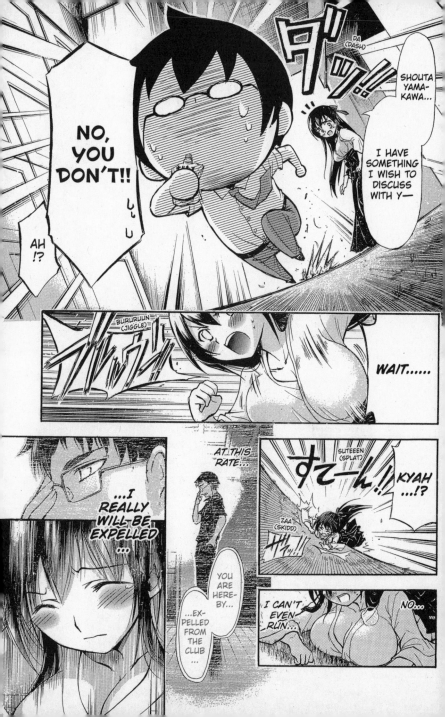

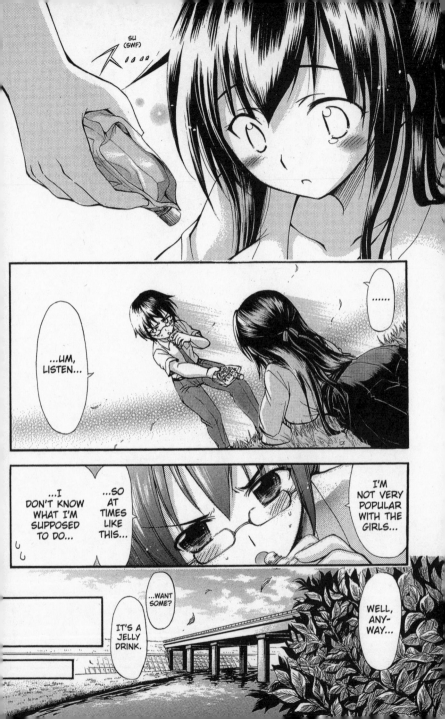

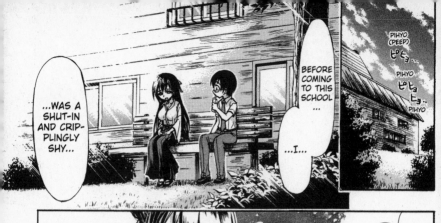

...BEFORE COMING TO THIS SCHOOL...

...WAS A SHUT-IN AND CRIPPLINGLY SHY...

PIHYO (PEEP)

PIHYO

PIHYO

...I...

WH—

WHAT'S SO SURPRISING ABOUT IT!!?

HUH?

REALLY? THAT'S SURPRISING TO HEAR...

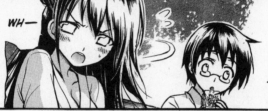

THIS IS THE FIRST TIME...

...I'VE EVER SPOKEN TO A MAN OTHER THAN MY MASTER...

KAAAA (BLUUUSH)

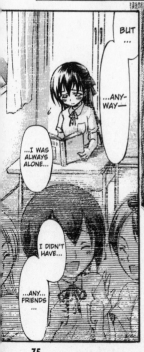

BUT...

...ANY-WAY—

...I WAS ALWAYS ALONE...

I DIDN'T HAVE...

...ANY... FRIENDS...

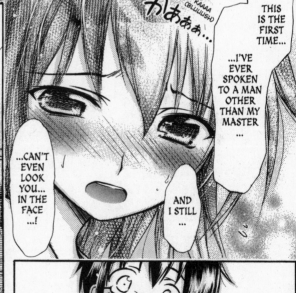

...CAN'T EVEN LOOK YOU... IN THE FACE...!

AND I STILL...

75

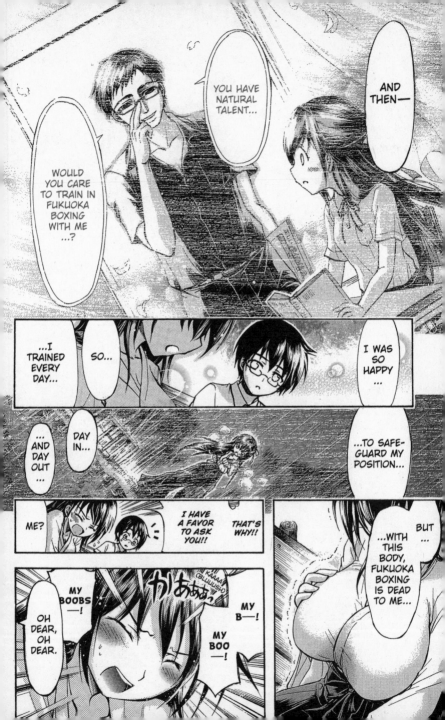

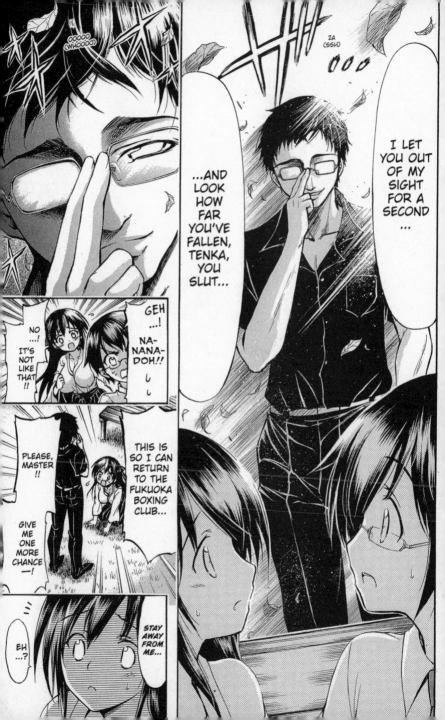

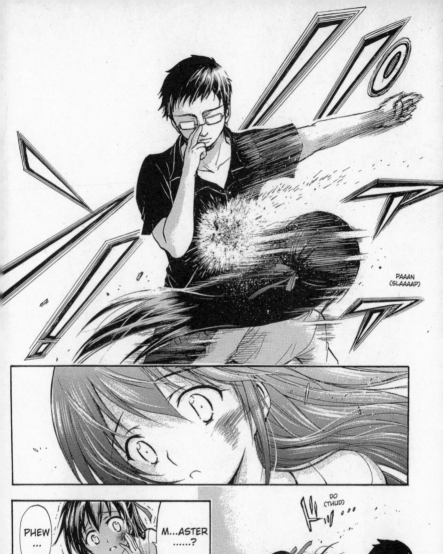

PAAAN
(SLAAAAP)

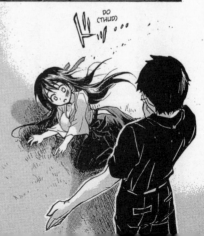

DO
(THUD)

PHEW
...

M...ASTER
......?

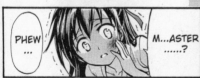

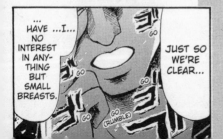

... HAVE ...I... NO INTEREST IN ANY- THING BUT SMALL BREASTS.

JUST SO WE'RE CLEAR...

GO
GO
GO
GO
GO
GO
(RUMBLE)

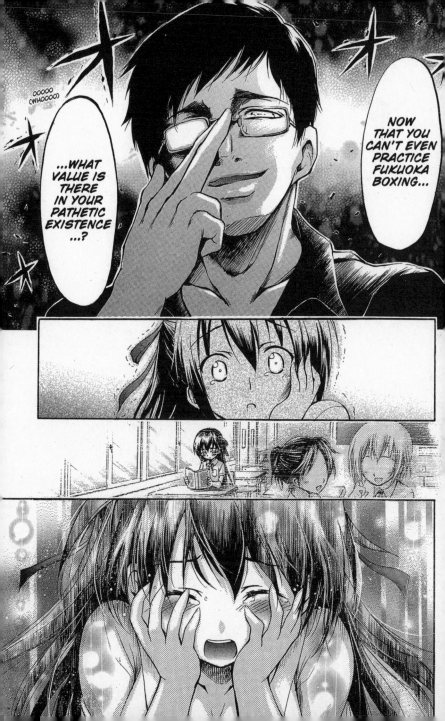

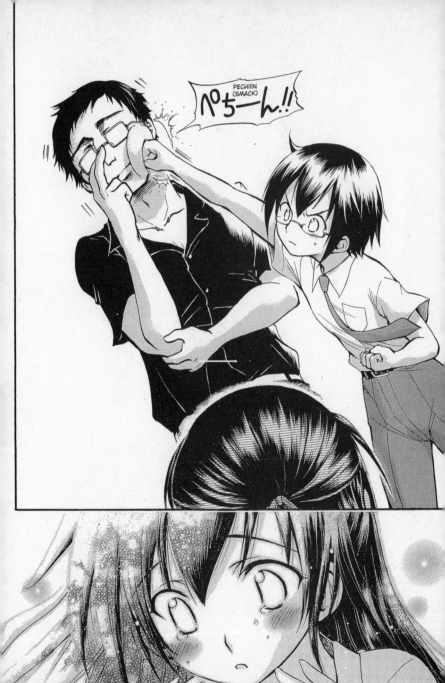

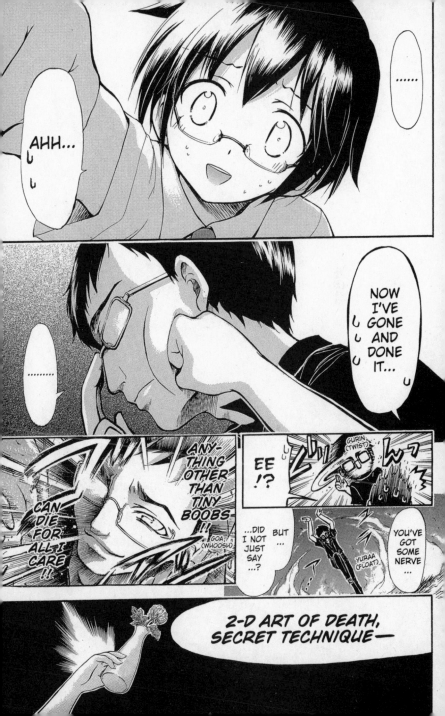

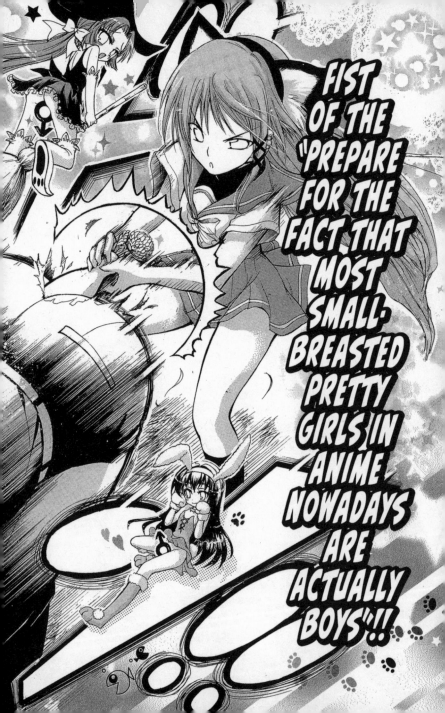

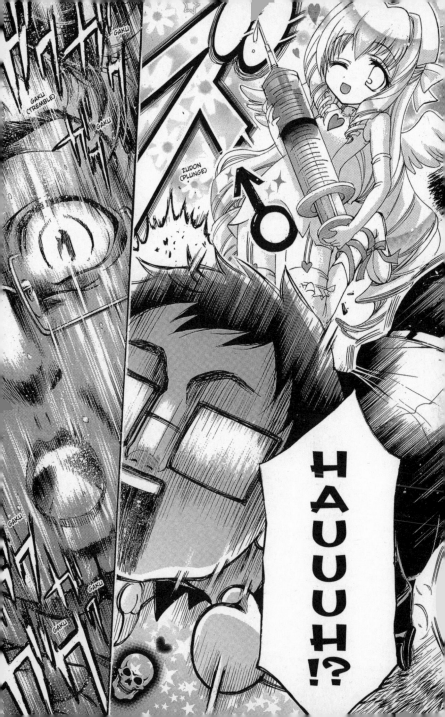

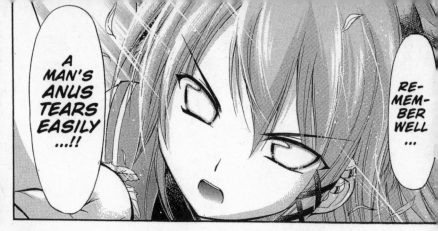

A MAN'S ANUS TEARS EASILY...!!

RE-MEM-BER WELL...

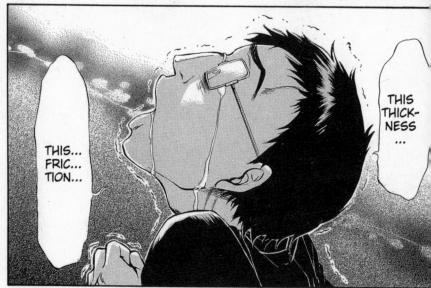

THIS... FRIC... TION...

THIS THICK-NESS...

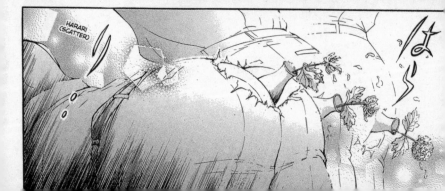

HARARI
(SCATTER)

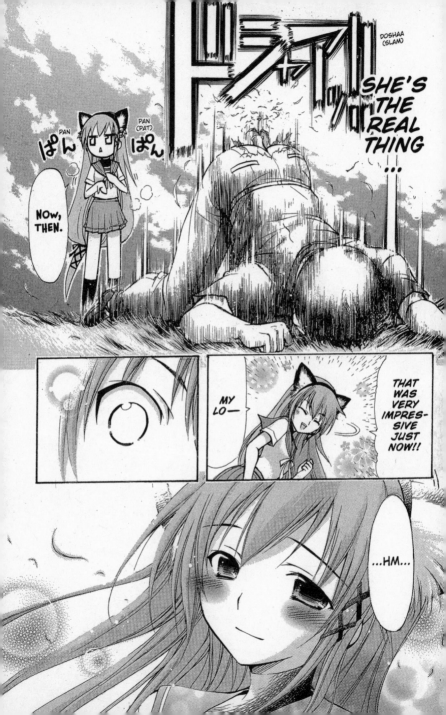

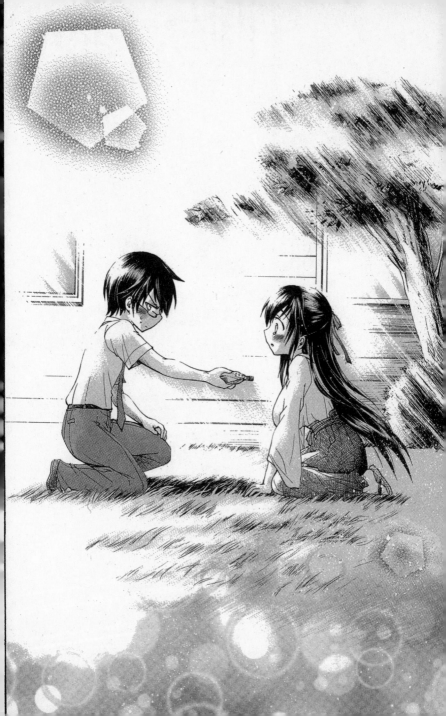

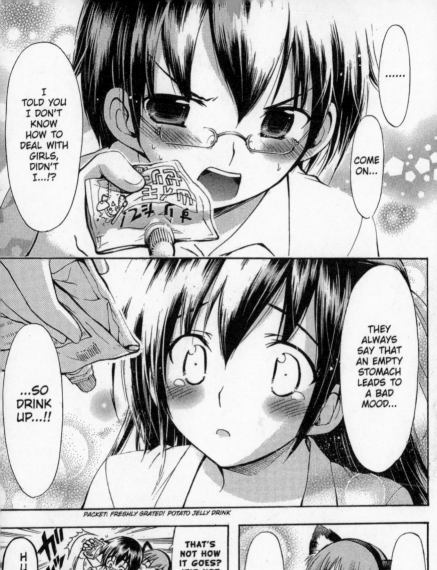

I TOLD YOU I DON'T KNOW HOW TO DEAL WITH GIRLS, DIDN'T I...!?

......

COME ON...

...SO DRINK UP...!!

THEY ALWAYS SAY THAT AN EMPTY STOMACH LEADS TO A BAD MOOD...

PACKET: FRESHLY GRATED! POTATO JELLY DRINK

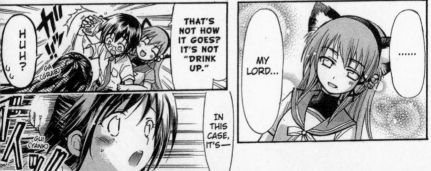

HUH?

THAT'S NOT HOW IT GOES? IT'S NOT "DRINK UP."

......

MY LORD...

IN THIS CASE, IT'S—

GA! (GRAB)

GUI (YANK)

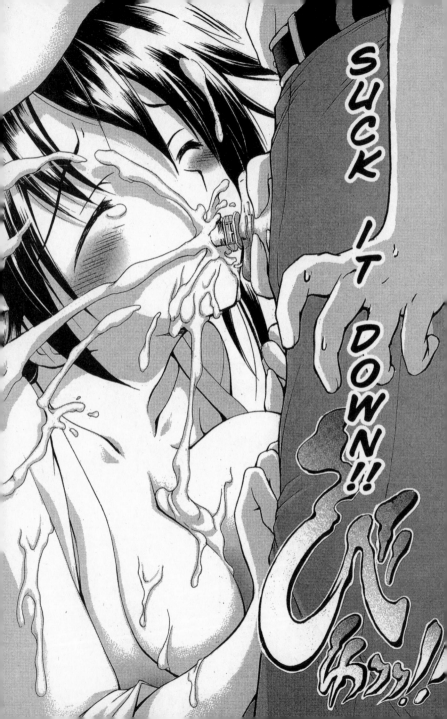

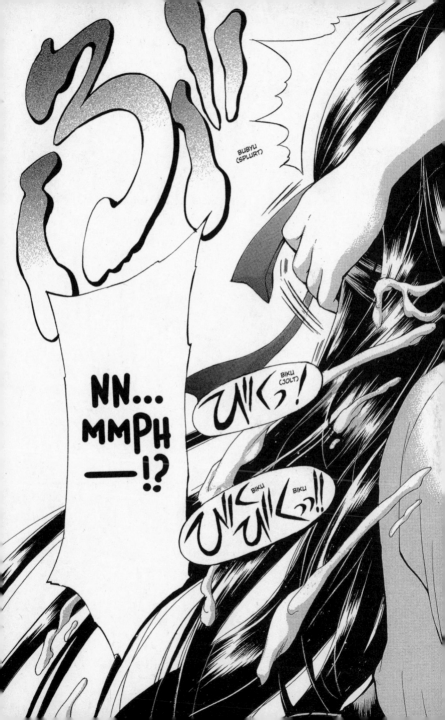

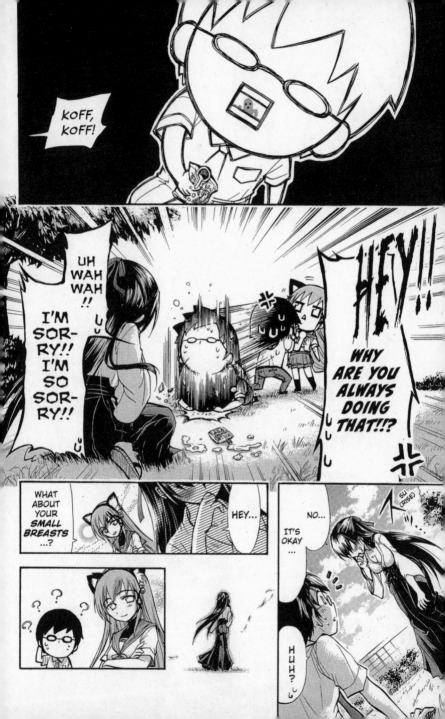

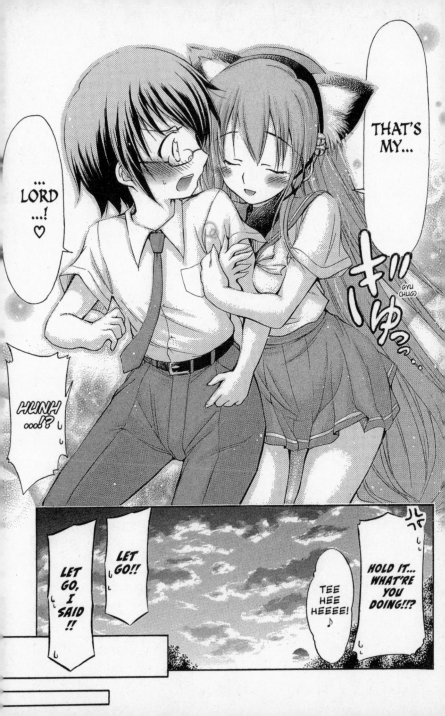

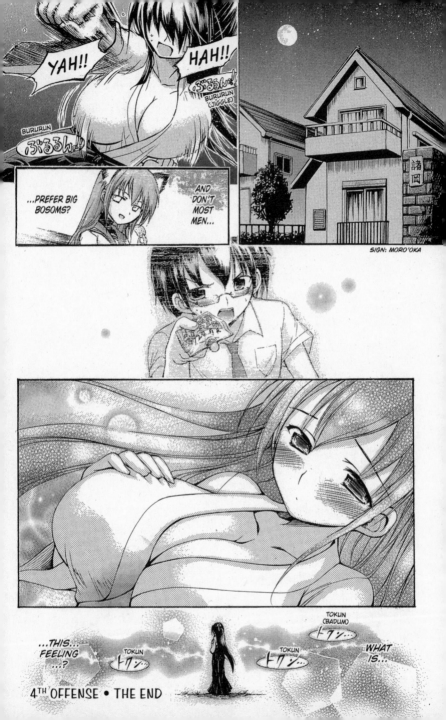

SIGN: MORO'OKA

4ᵀᴴ OFFENSE • THE END

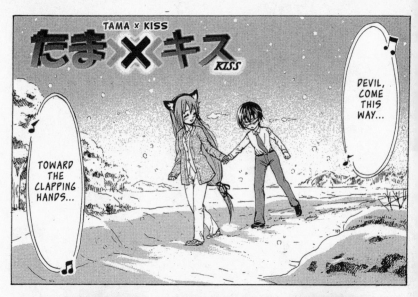

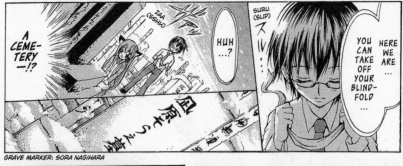

GRAVE MARKER: SORA NAGIHARA

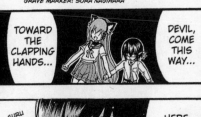

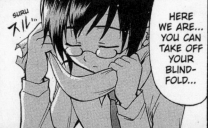

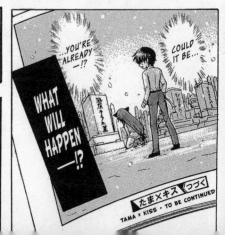

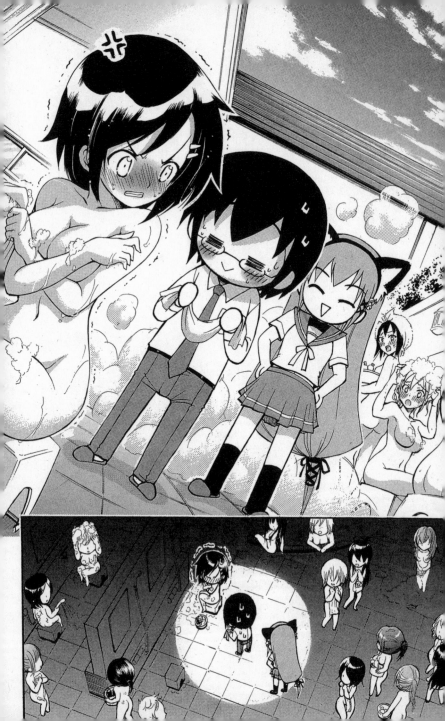

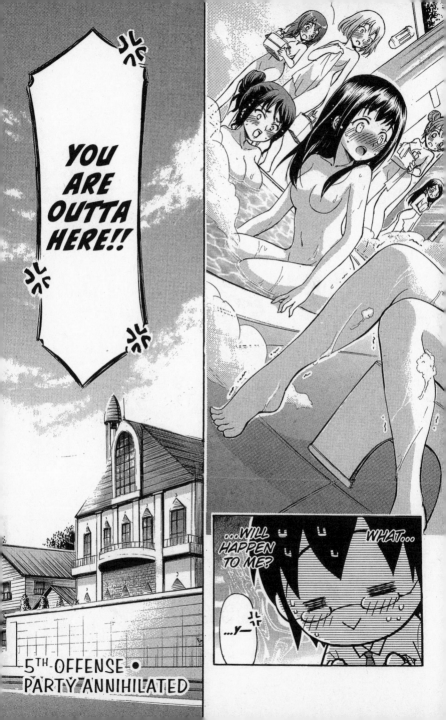

5TH OFFENSE •
PARTY ANNIHILATED

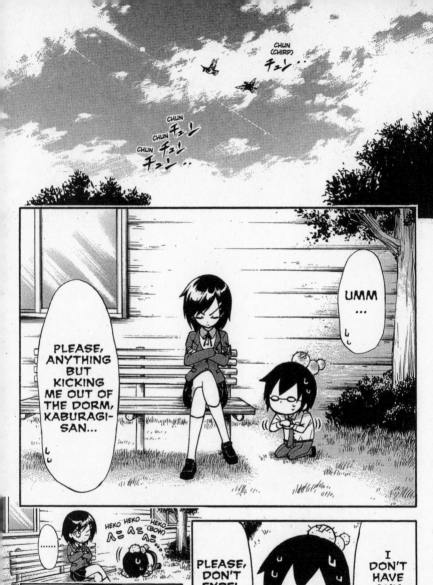

CHUN
(CHIRP)
チュン‥

CHUN
CHUN チュン
CHUN チュン
チュン‥

UMM
...

PLEASE,
ANYTHING
BUT
KICKING
ME OUT OF
THE DORM,
KABURAGI-
SAN...

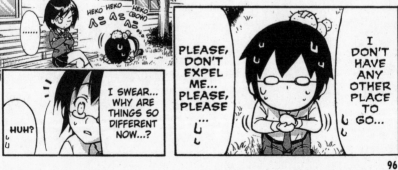

......

HEKO HEKO HEKO
(BOW)

PLEASE,
DON'T
EXPEL
ME...
PLEASE,
PLEASE

I
DON'T
HAVE
ANY
OTHER
PLACE
TO
GO...

HUH?

I SWEAR...
WHY ARE
THINGS SO
DIFFERENT
NOW...?

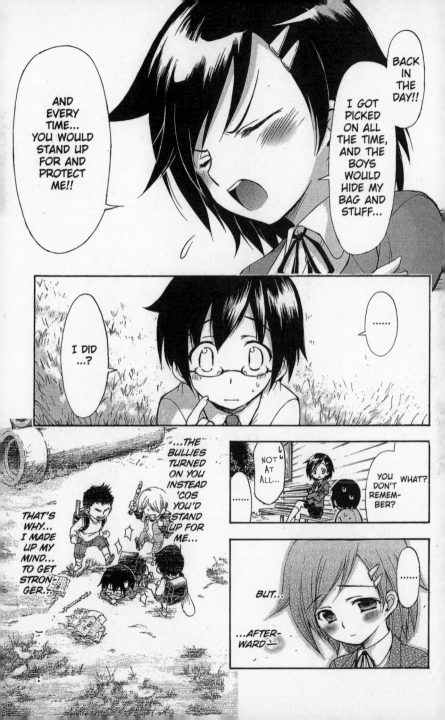

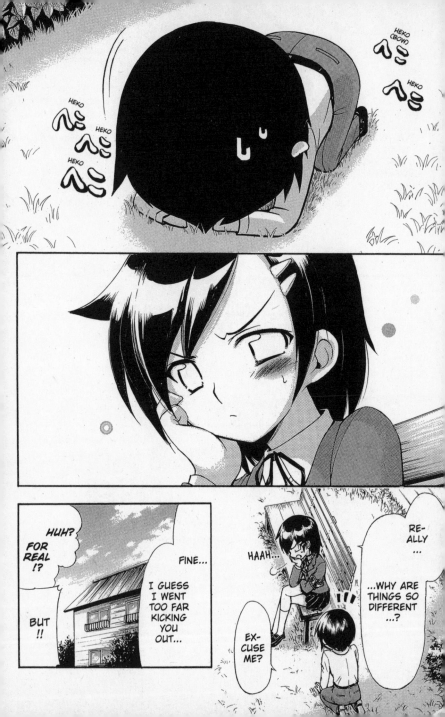

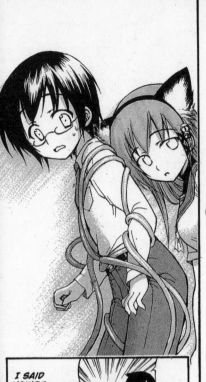

GET
OUUUT
—!!

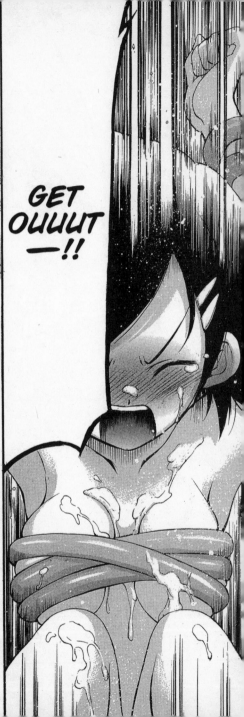

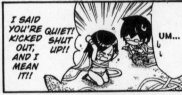

I SAID YOU'RE KICKED OUT, AND I MEAN IT!!

QUIET! SHUT UP!!

UM...

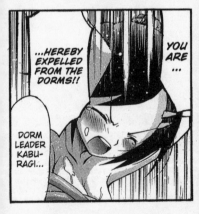

...HEREBY EXPELLED FROM THE DORMS!!

YOU ARE...

DORM LEADER KABURAGI...

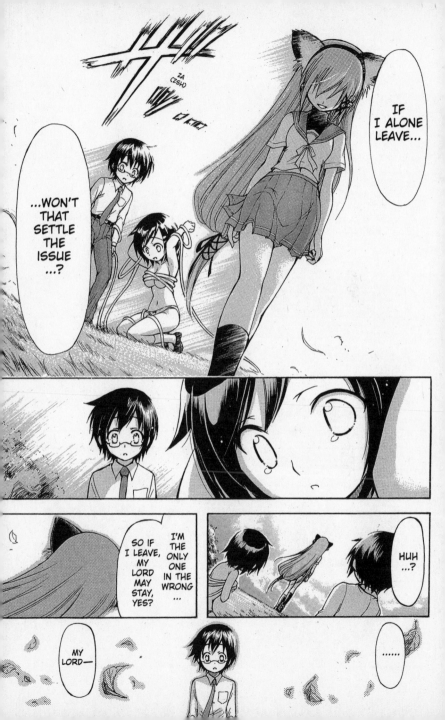

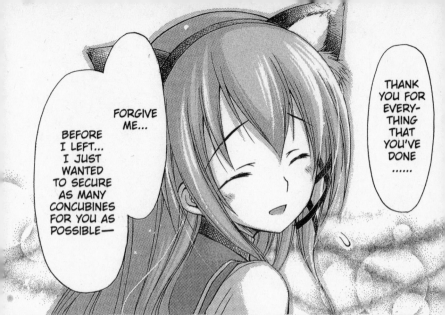

THANK YOU FOR EVERY-THING THAT YOU'VE DONE ......

FORGIVE ME...

BEFORE I LEFT... I JUST WANTED TO SECURE AS MANY CONCUBINES FOR YOU AS POSSIBLE—

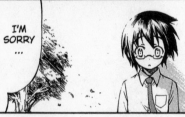

I'M SORRY...

I PROMISE I WON'T BE BOTHERING YOU... AGAIN—

BUT IT LOOKS LIKE THAT ONLY CAUSED YOU MORE TROUBLE...

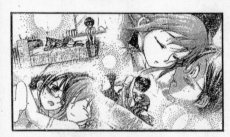

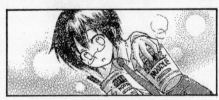

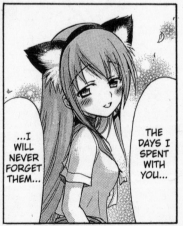

...I WILL NEVER FORGET THEM...

THE DAYS I SPENT WITH YOU...

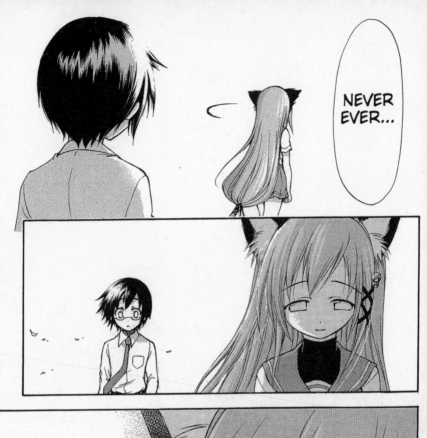

NEVER
EVER...

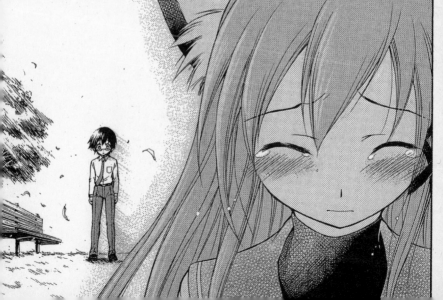

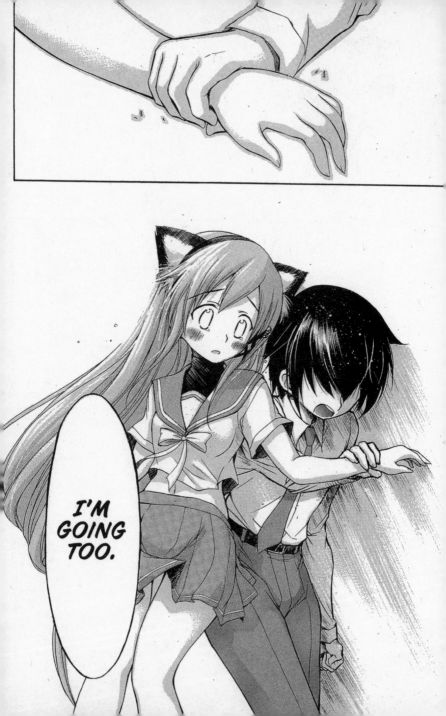

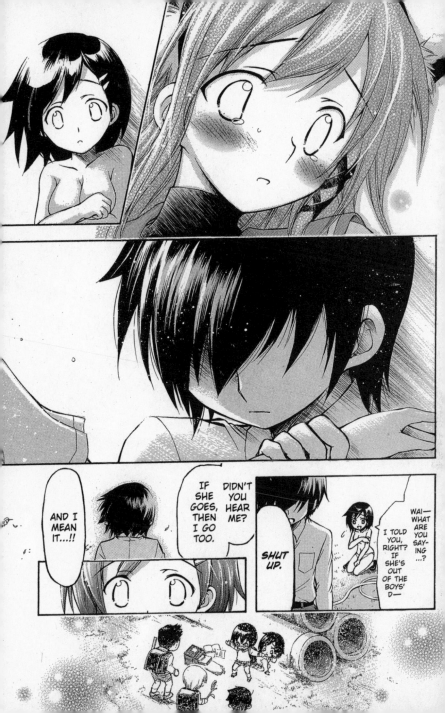

AND I MEAN IT...!!

IF SHE GOES, THEN I GO TOO.

DIDN'T YOU HEAR ME?

SHUT UP.

I TOLD YOU, RIGHT? IF SHE'S OUT OF THE BOYS' D—

WAI—WHAT ARE YOU SAYING...?

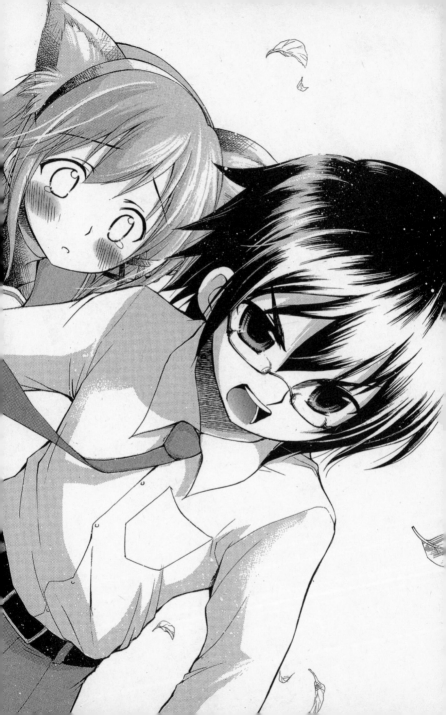

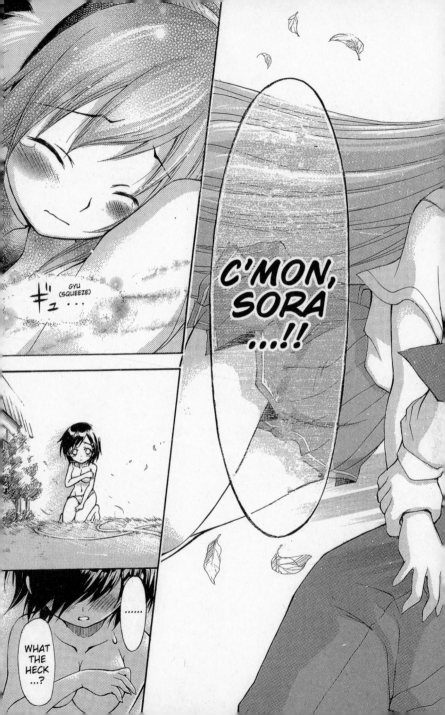

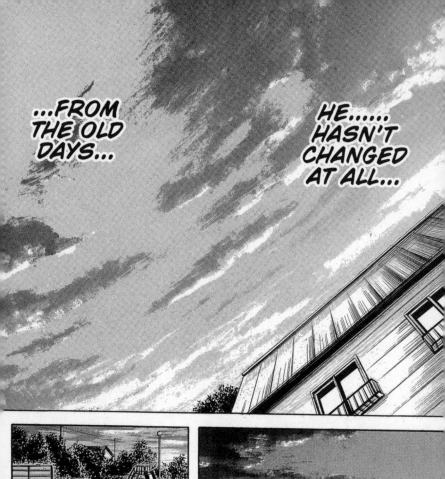

...FROM THE OLD DAYS...

HE...... HASN'T CHANGED AT ALL...

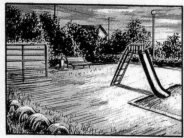

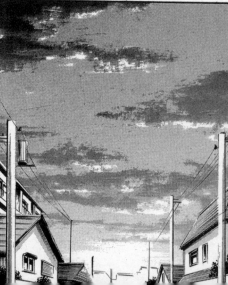

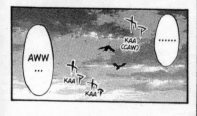

AWW...

KAA?
KAA?

KAA?
(CAW)

......

....

NOW I'VE DONE IT...

IS THIS WHAT I THINK IT IS!? I'M HOMELESS NOW!? IN THE MIDDLE OF WINTER!?

MY LORD...

WHERE AM I S'POSED TO SLEEP NOW!?

WHAT DO I DO? I'M SUCH AN IDIOT!!

...SKIN-TO-SKIN LIKE THIS—

IF WE WARM EACH OTHER UP...

DON'T FRET...

SU (SWF)

HUH ...?

HEY!?

HEY...

WAIT!!

HUNH ...!?

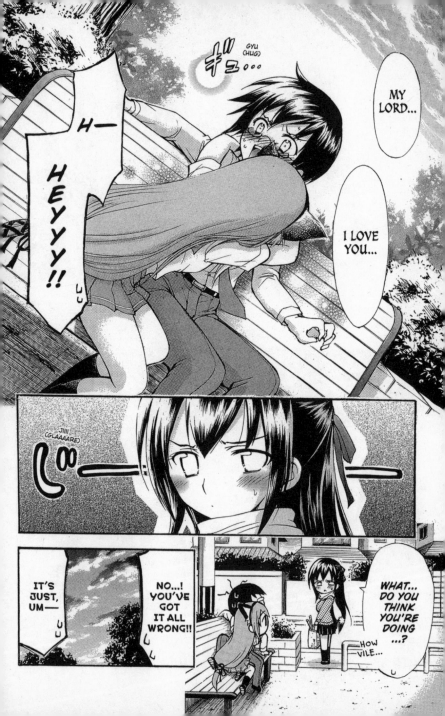

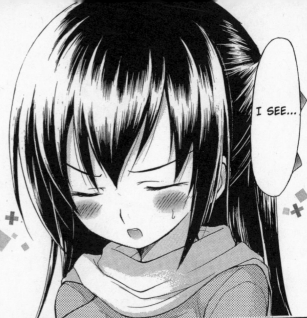

I SEE...

SO YOU'VE BEEN THROWN OUT OF THE DORMS AND HAVE NO PLACE TO GO...

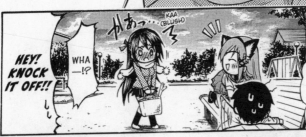

HEY! KNOCK IT OFF!!

WHA—!?

KAA (BLUSH)

INDEED! THAT'S WHY MY LORD AND I ARE WARMING EACH OTHER UP WITH OUR BODIES! ♪

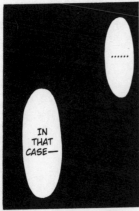

......

IN THAT CASE—

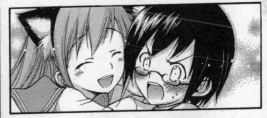

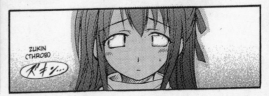

ZUKIN (THROB)

117

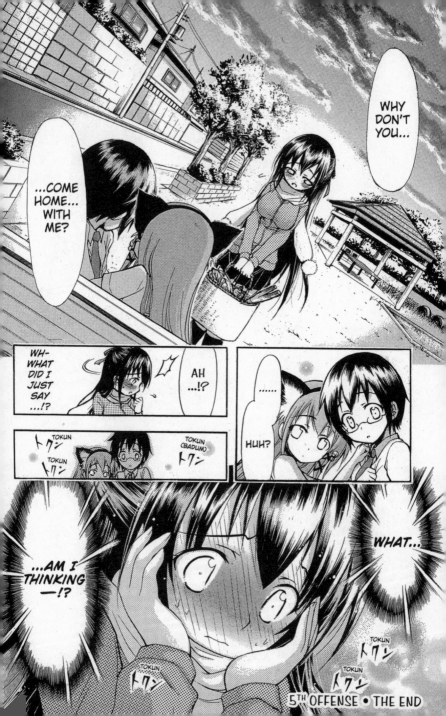

WHY DON'T YOU...

...COME HOME... WITH ME?

WH-WHAT DID I JUST SAY...!?

AH...!?

......

HUH?

TOKUN
TOKUN

TOKUN
(BADUM)

WHAT...

...AM I THINKING —!?

TOKUN

TOKUN

TOKUN

5TH OFFENSE • THE END

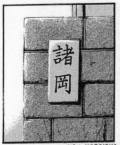

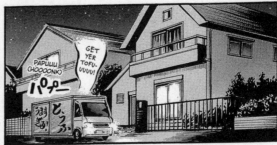

PAPULUU (HOOOONK) パブー

GET YER TOFU-UUU!

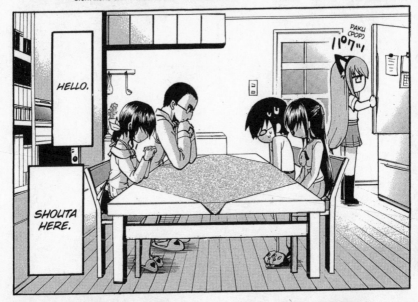

PAKU (POP) パッ

HELLO.

SHOUTA HERE.

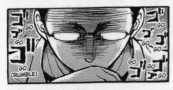

GO GO GO GO GO GO GO GO GO GO (RUMBLE)

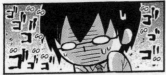

GO GO GO GO GO GO GO GO GO GO GO

TENKA MORO'OKA OFFERED TO LET ME STAY AT HER PLACE, AND HERE WE ARE, BUT—

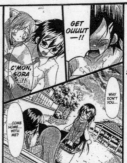

GET OUUUT—!!

C'MON, SORA...!!

WHY DON'T YOU...

...COME HOME... WITH ME?

'COS OF VARIOUS CIRCUMSTANCES, I GOT KICKED OUT OF THE DORM.

6TH OFFENSE • YOUR PROGRESS HAS BEEN LOST

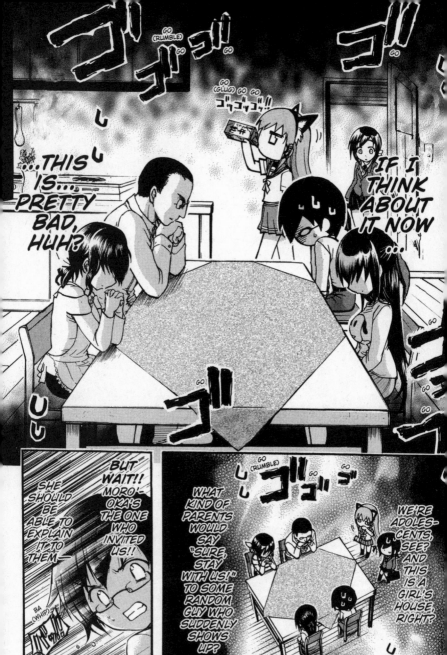

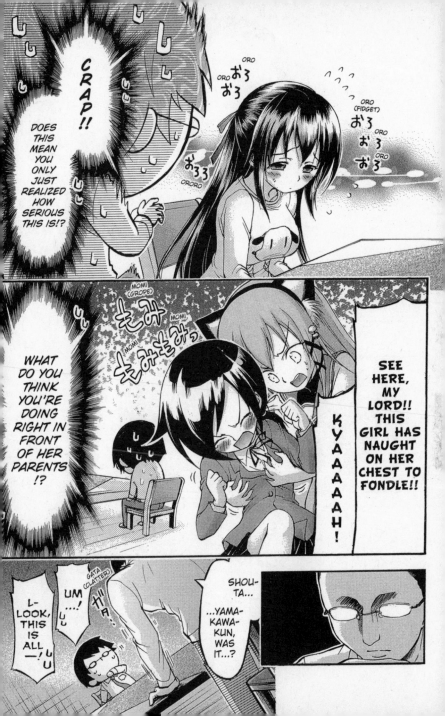

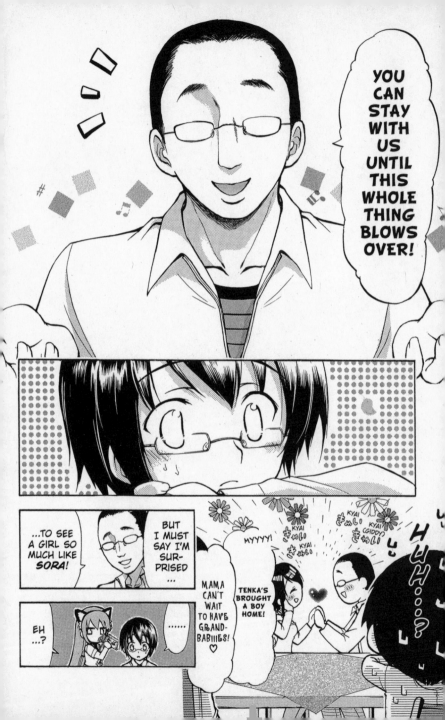

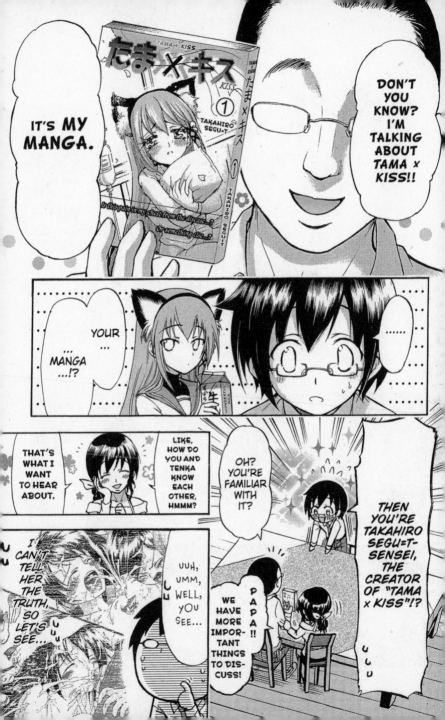

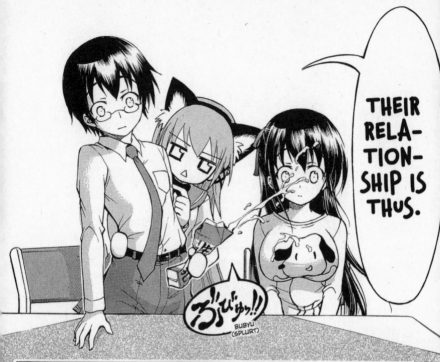

THEIR RELATIONSHIP IS THUS.

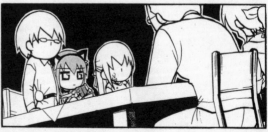

ぶびゅっ!!
BUBYU
(SPLURT)

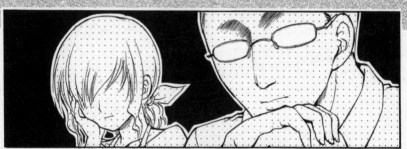

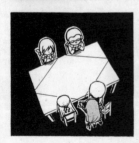

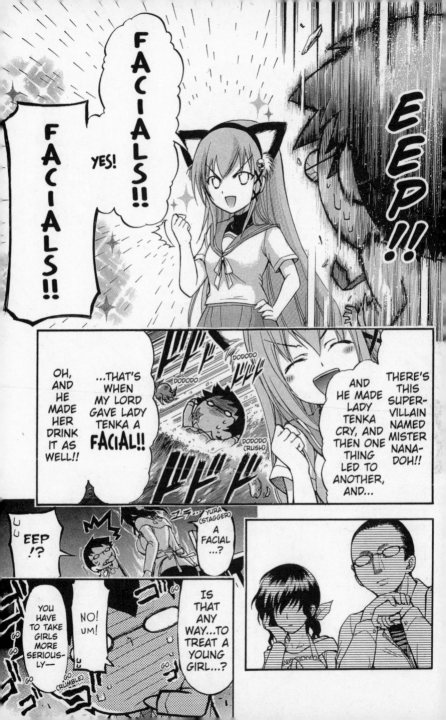

FACIALS!!

FACIALS!!

FACIALS!!

YES!

EEP!!

THERE'S THIS SUPER-VILLAIN NAMED MISTER NANA-DOH!!

AND HE MADE LADY TENKA CRY, AND THEN ONE THING LED TO ANOTHER, AND...

...THAT'S WHEN MY LORD GAVE LADY TENKA A FACIAL!!

OH, AND HE MADE HER DRINK IT AS WELL!!

DODODO

DODODO (CRUSH)

EEP!?

YURA (STAGGER)

A FACIAL...?

YOU HAVE TO TAKE GIRLS MORE SERIOUS-LY—

NO! UM!

IS THAT ANY WAY...TO TREAT A YOUNG GIRL...?

GO GO GO (CRUMBLE)

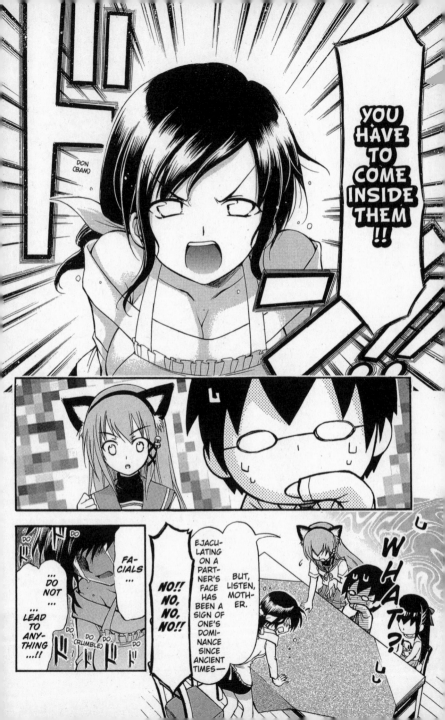

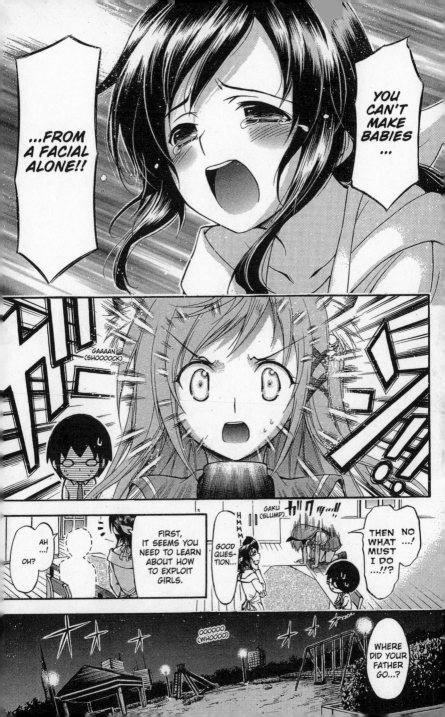

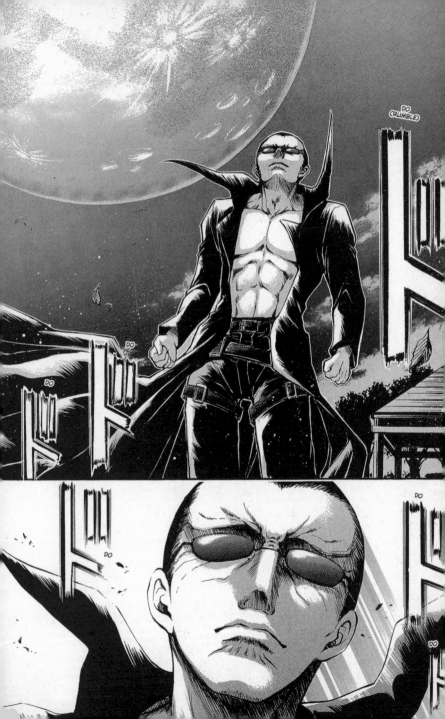

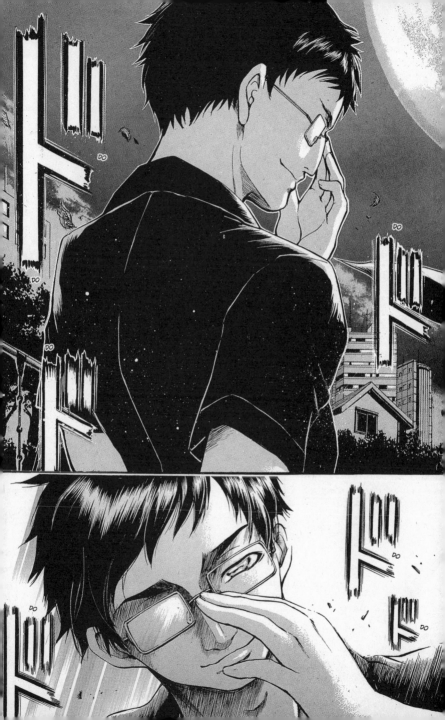

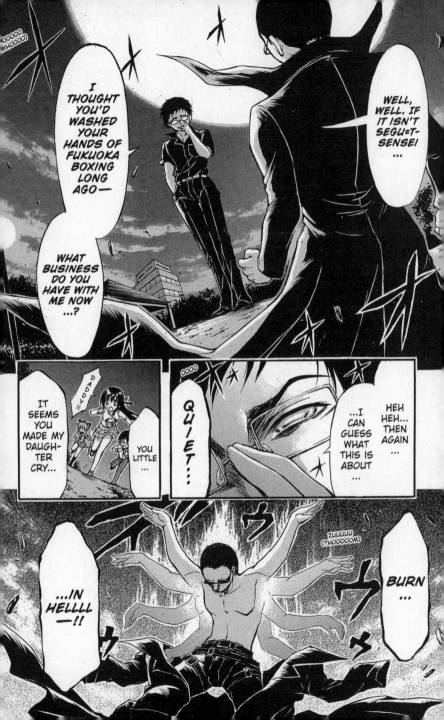

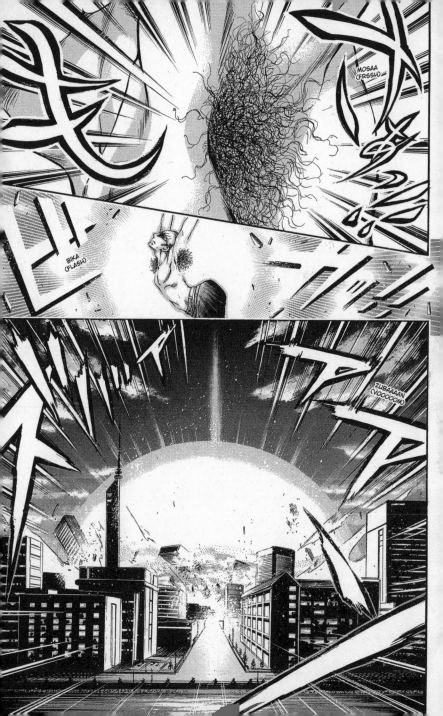

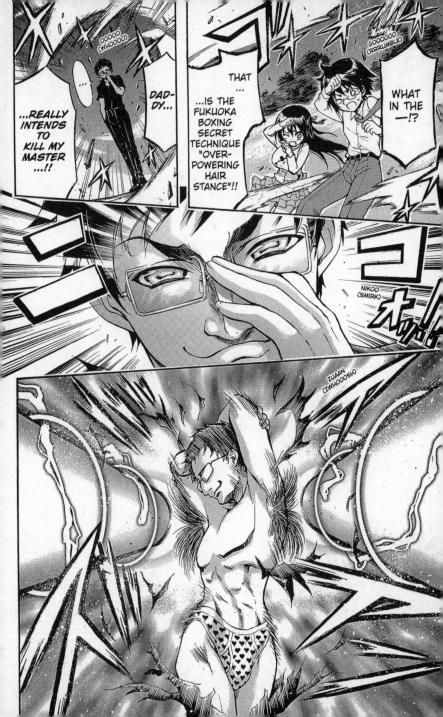

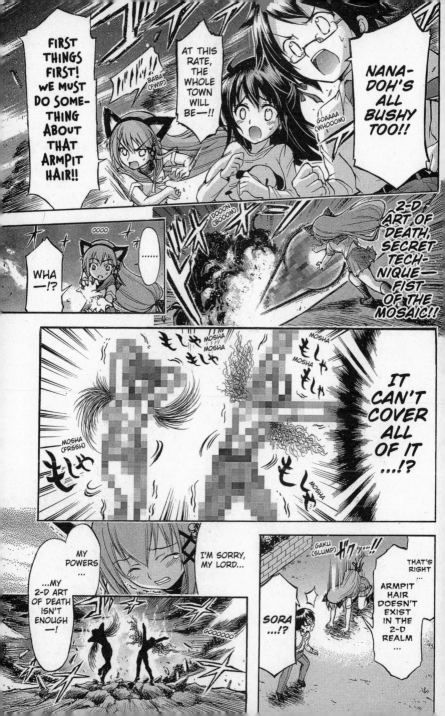

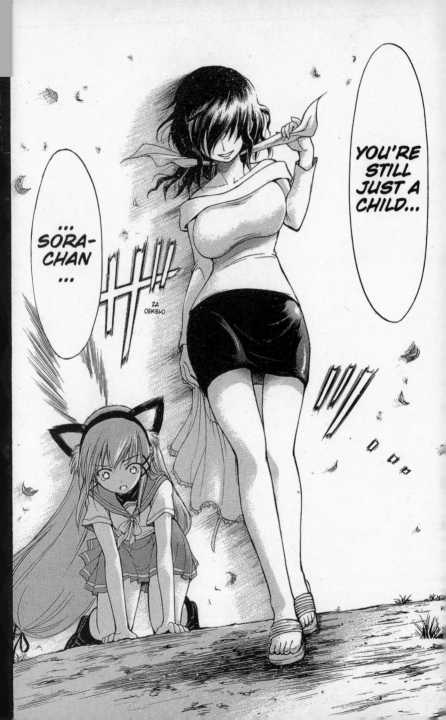

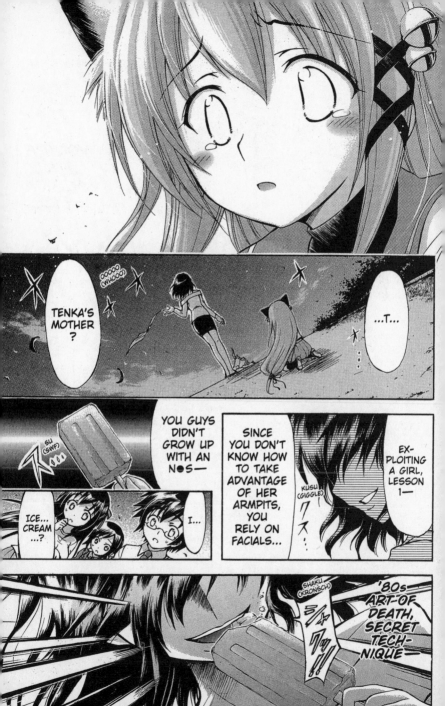

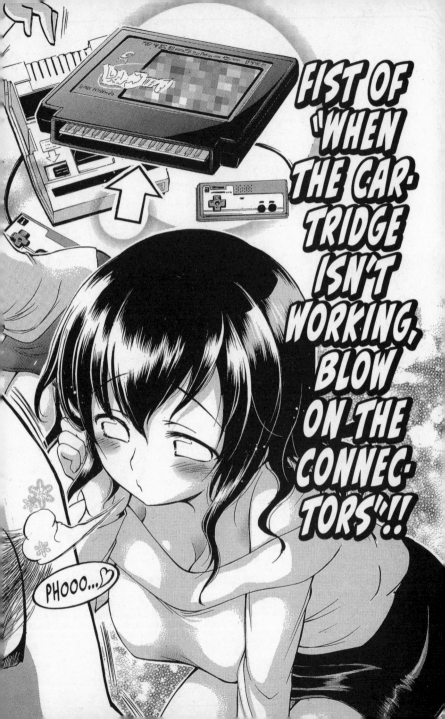

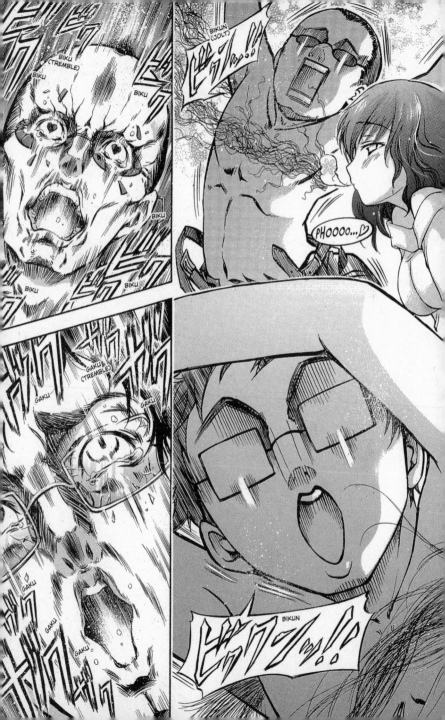

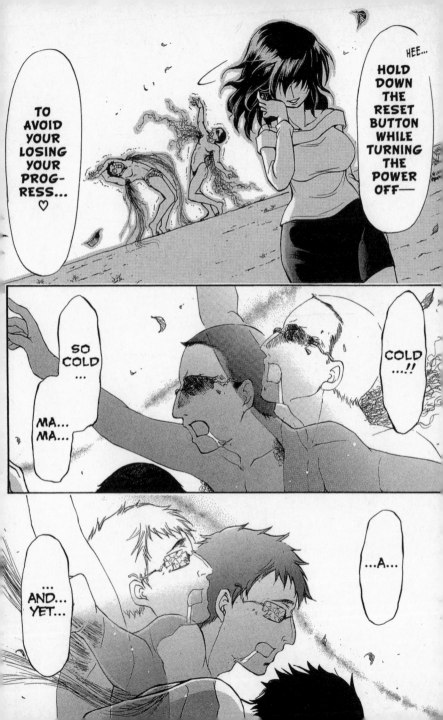

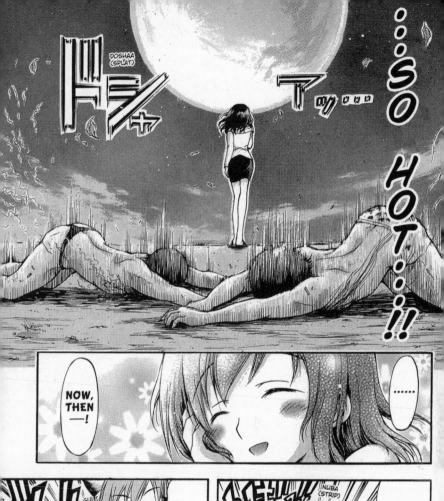

...SO HOT...!!

NOW, THEN —!

......

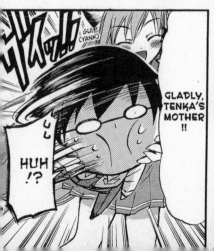

HUH !?

GUI! (CYANK)

GLADLY, TENKA'S MOTHER !!

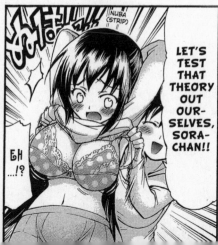

NUBA (STRIP)

EH ....!?

LET'S TEST THAT THEORY OUT OUR-SELVES, SORA-CHAN!!

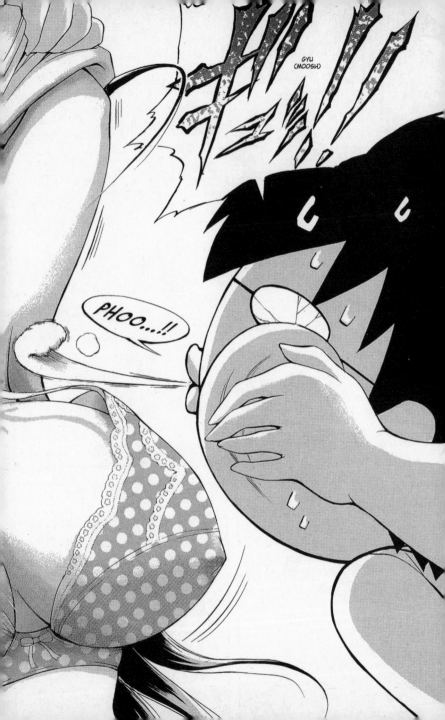

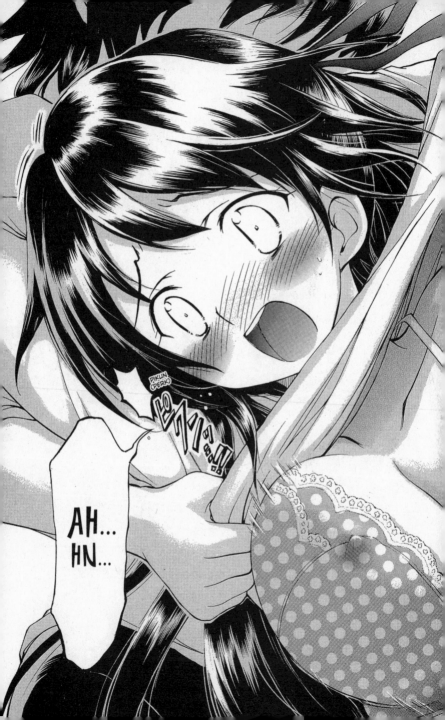

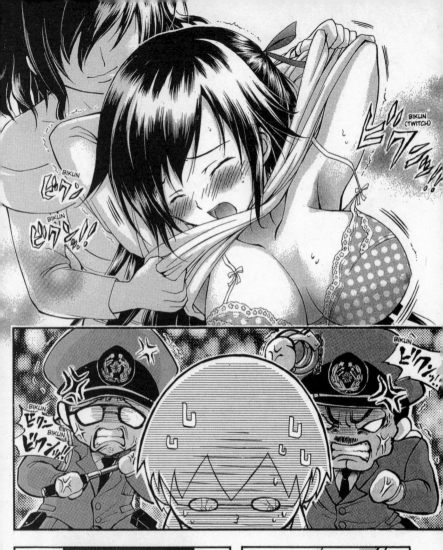

BIKUN (TWITCH)

BIKUN

BIKUN

BIKUN

BIKUN

BIKUN

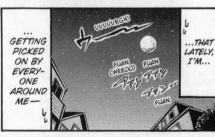

...GETTING PICKED ON BY EVERY-ONE AROUND ME—

UUUUURGH!

FUAN (WEEOO) FUAN

FUAN

...THAT LATELY, I'M...

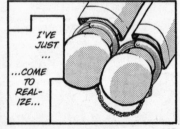

I'VE JUST...

...COME TO REAL-IZE...

6TH OFFENSE • THE END

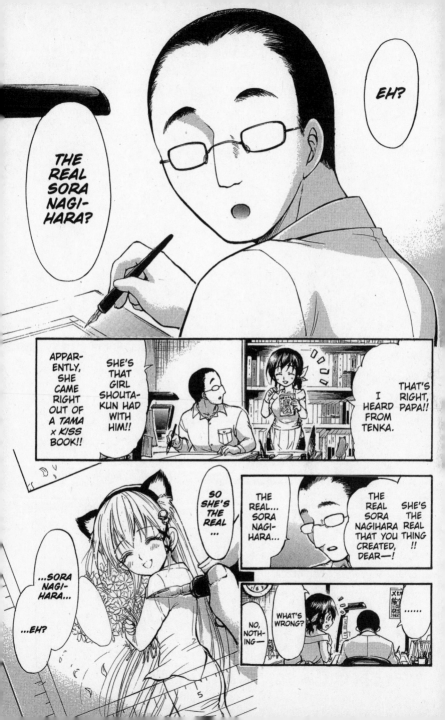

EH?

THE REAL SORA NAGI-HARA?

APPAR-ENTLY, SHE CAME RIGHT OUT OF A *TAMA x KISS* BOOK!!

SHE'S THAT GIRL SHOUTA-KUN HAD WITH HIM!!

I HEARD FROM TENKA.

THAT'S RIGHT, PAPA!!

...SORA NAGI-HARA...

...EH?

SO SHE'S THE REAL

THE REAL... SORA NAGI-HARA...

THE REAL SORA NAGIHARA THAT YOU CREATED, DEAR—!

SHE'S THE REAL THING !!

NO, NOTHING—

WHAT'S WRONG?

......

5

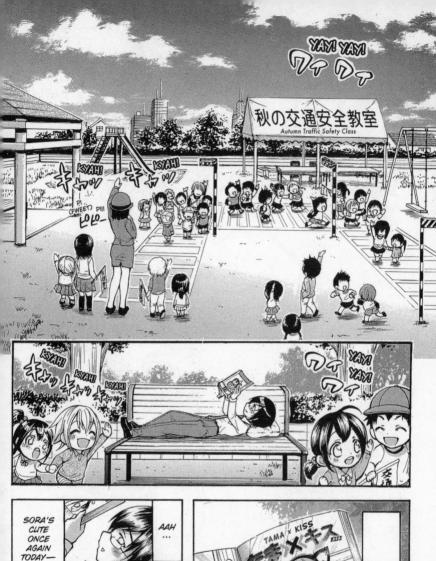

秋の交通安全教室
Autumn Traffic Safety Class

YAY! YAY!
ワイ ワイ

KYAH!
キャッ

KYAH!
キャッ

PI
(TWEET P!!!
ピ ピ ピ ー

KYAH!
キャッ

KYAH!
キャッ

KYAH!
キャッ

YAY!
YAY!
ワイ
ワイ

SORA'S
CUTE
ONCE
AGAIN
TODAY—

AAH
...

チラ...
CHIRA
(GLANCE)

THIS IS
SHOU-
TA.

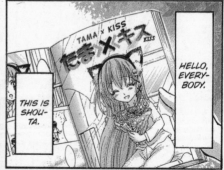

TAMA × KISS
たま×キス KISS

HELLO,
EVERY-
BODY.

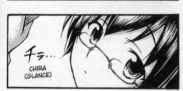

7TH OFFENSE • THE REAL THING?

144

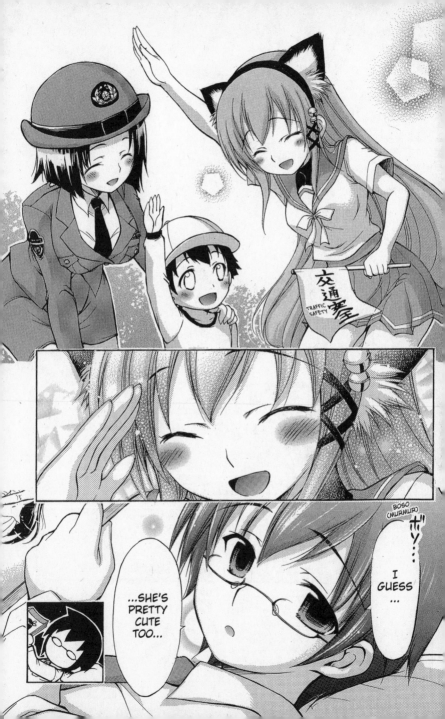

交通安全
TRAFFIC SAFETY

BOSO
(MURMUR)

...SHE'S PRETTY CUTE TOO...

I GUESS...

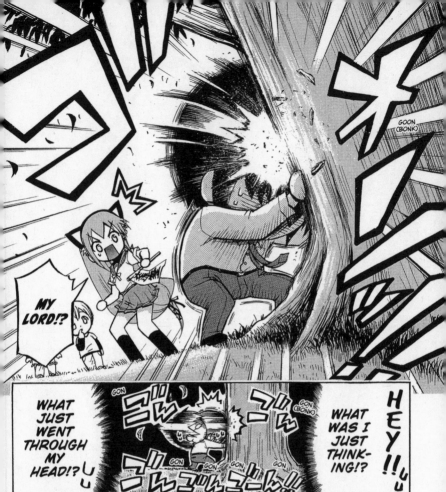

MY LORD!?

GOON
(BONK)

WHAT JUST WENT THROUGH MY HEAD!?

WHAT WAS I JUST THINK-ING!?

HEY!!

GON

GON (BONK)

GON GON GON

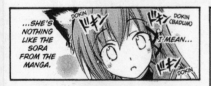

...SHE'S NOTHING LIKE THE SORA FROM THE MANGA.

DOKIN

DOKIN (BADUM)

I MEAN...

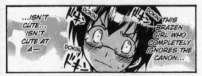

...ISN'T CUTE... ISN'T CUTE AT A—

THIS BRAZEN GIRL WHO COMPLETELY IGNORES THE CANON...

DOKIN

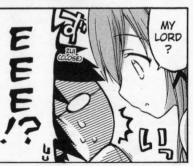

MY LORD?

ZUI (CLOSE)

EEE!?

146

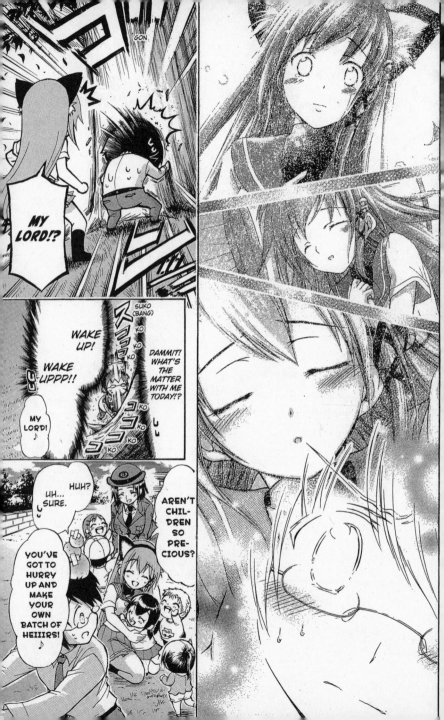

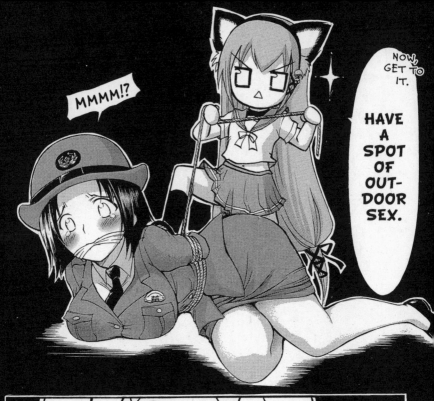

MMMM!?

NOW, GET TO IT.

HAVE A SPOT OF OUTDOOR SEX.

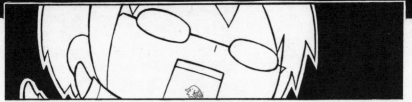

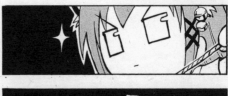

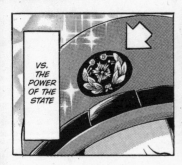

VS. THE POWER OF THE STATE

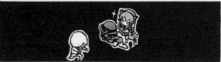

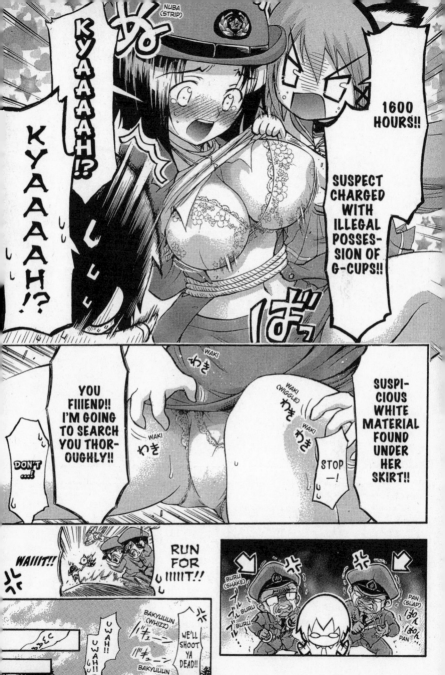

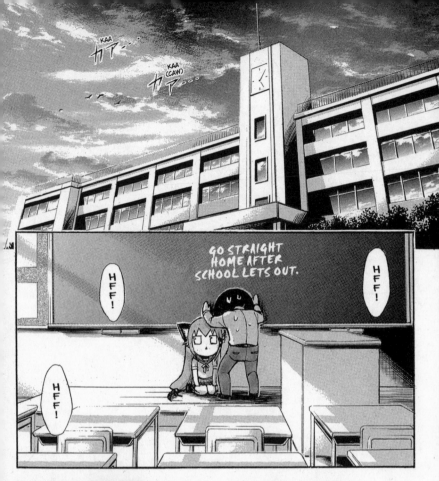

GO STRAIGHT HOME AFTER SCHOOL LETS OUT.

HFF!

HFF!

HFF!

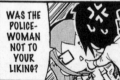

WAS THE POLICE-WOMAN NOT TO YOUR LIKING?

I ALMOST GOT ARRESTED AGAIIIIN!!

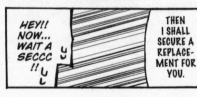

HEY!! NOW... WAIT A SECCC!!

THEN I SHALL SECURE A REPLACE-MENT FOR YOU.

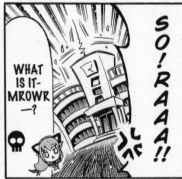

WHAT IS IT-MROWR—?

SO!RAAA!!

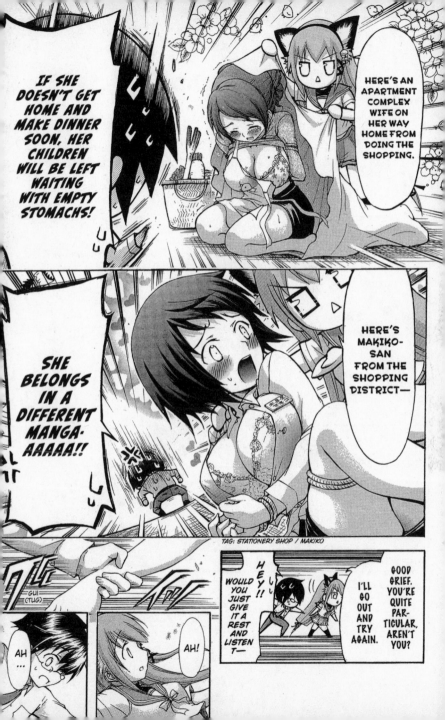

IF SHE DOESN'T GET HOME AND MAKE DINNER SOON, HER CHILDREN WILL BE LEFT WAITING WITH EMPTY STOMACHS!

HERE'S AN APARTMENT COMPLEX WIFE ON HER WAY HOME FROM DOING THE SHOPPING.

SHE BELONGS IN A DIFFERENT MANGA-AAAAA!!

HERE'S MAKIKO-SAN FROM THE SHOPPING DISTRICT—

TAG: STATIONERY SHOP / MAKIKO

GUI (TUG)

HEY!!

WOULD YOU JUST GIVE IT A REST AND LISTEN T—

I'LL GO OUT AND TRY AGAIN.

GOOD GRIEF. YOU'RE QUITE PARTICULAR, AREN'T YOU?

AH...

AH!

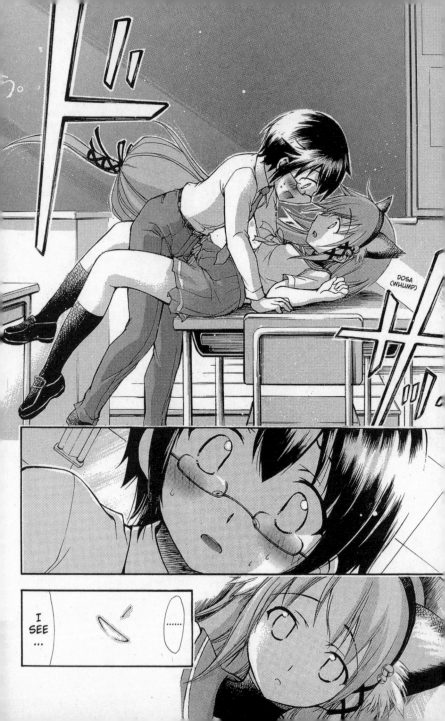

DOSA
(WHUMP)

I SEE
...

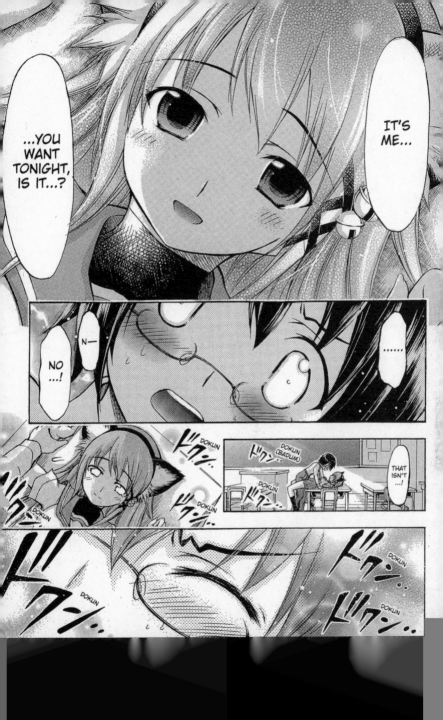

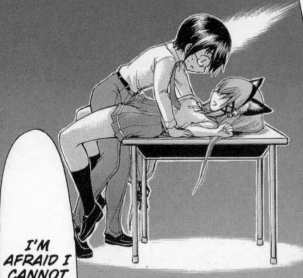

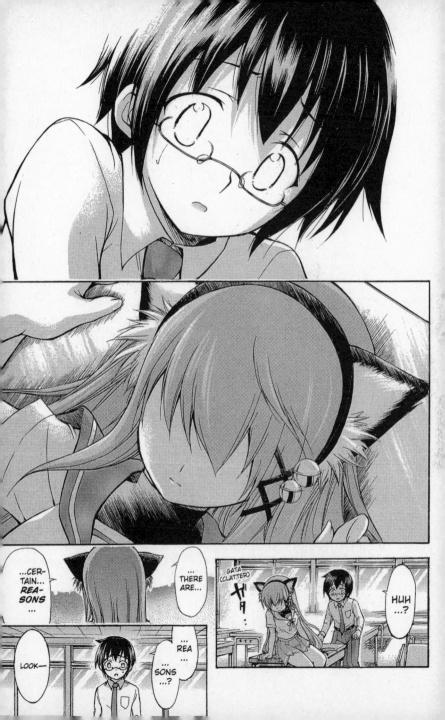

...CER-
TAIN...
REA-
SONS
...

...
THERE
ARE...

GATA
(CLATTER)

HUH
...?

LOOK—

...
REA
...
SONS
...?

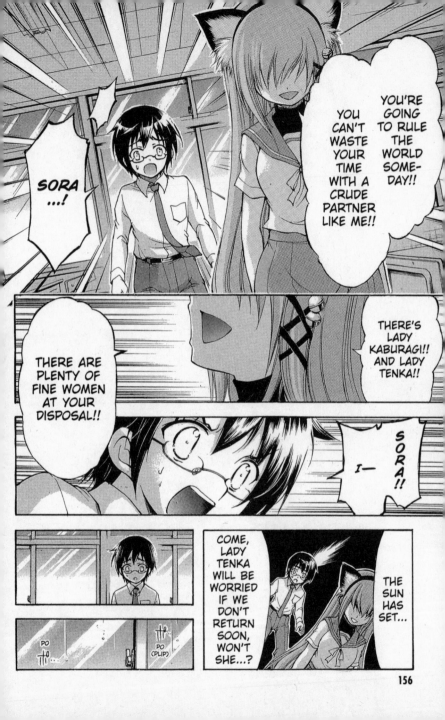

SORA...!

YOU'RE GOING TO RULE THE WORLD SOMEDAY!!

YOU CAN'T WASTE YOUR TIME WITH A CRUDE PARTNER LIKE ME!!

THERE'S LADY KABURAGI!! AND LADY TENKA!!

THERE ARE PLENTY OF FINE WOMEN AT YOUR DISPOSAL!!

I—

SORA!!

COME, LADY TENKA WILL BE WORRIED IF WE DON'T RETURN SOON, WON'T SHE...?

THE SUN HAS SET...

PO
PO
(PLIP)

156

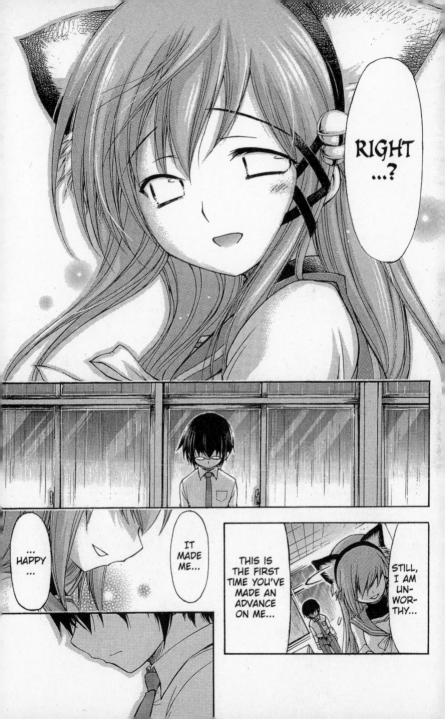

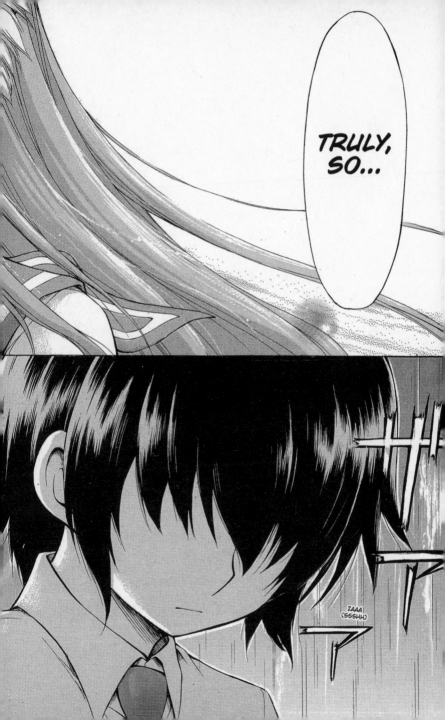

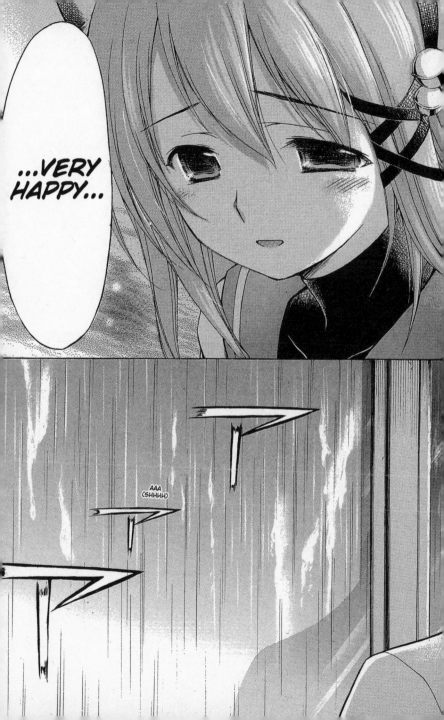

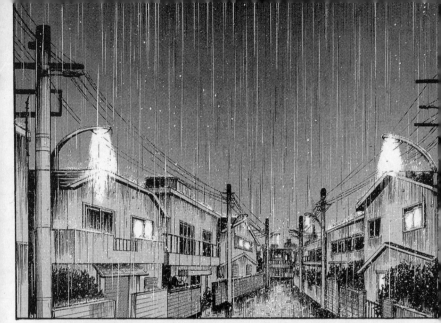

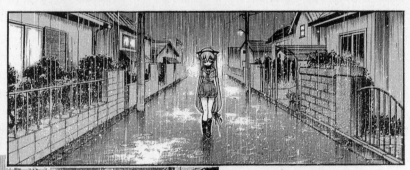

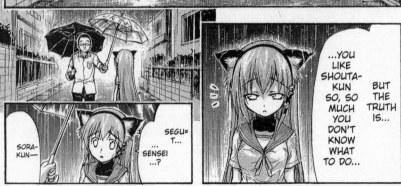

SORA-
KUN—

SEGU=
T...
...
SENSEI
...?

...YOU
LIKE
SHOUTA-
KUN
SO, SO
MUCH
YOU
DON'T
KNOW
WHAT
TO DO...

BUT
THE
TRUTH
IS...

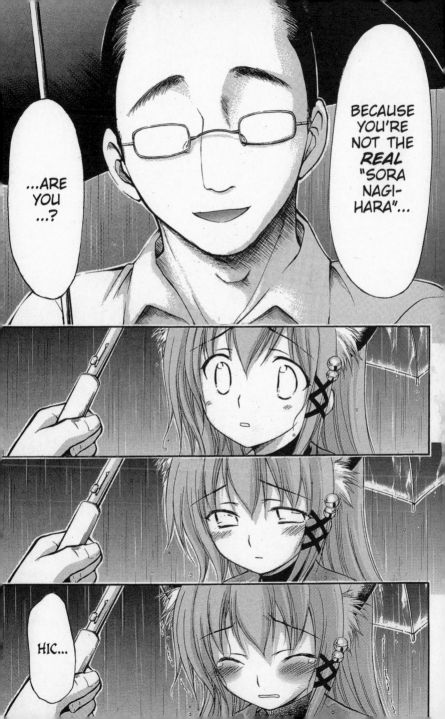

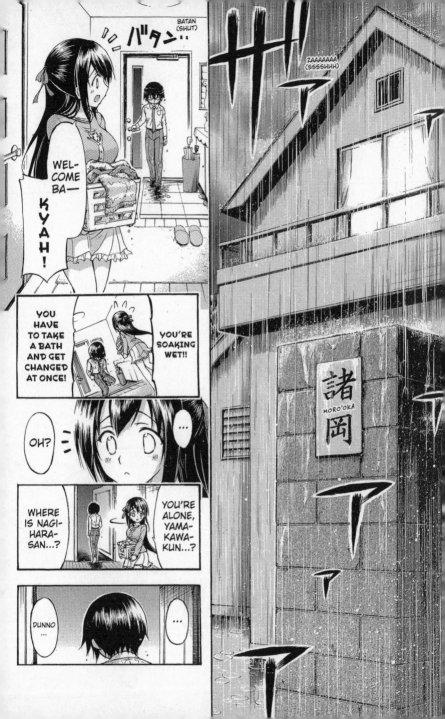

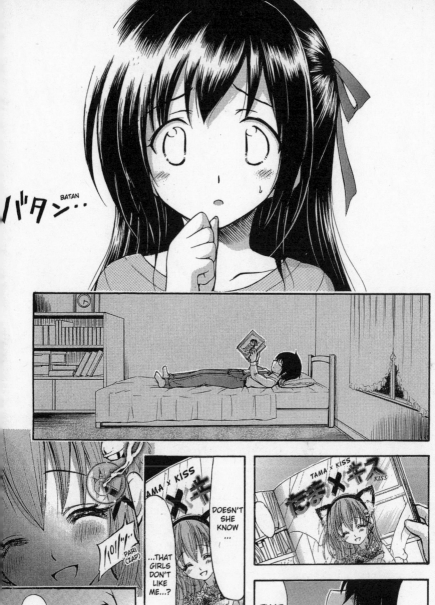

バタン‥ BATAN

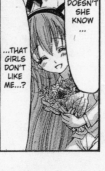

TAMA × KISS

DOESN'T
SHE
KNOW
...

...THAT
GIRLS
DON'T
LIKE
ME...?

TAMA × KISS
KISS

PARI
CLAP!

THAT
IDIOT
...

....

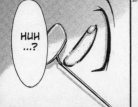

HUH
...?

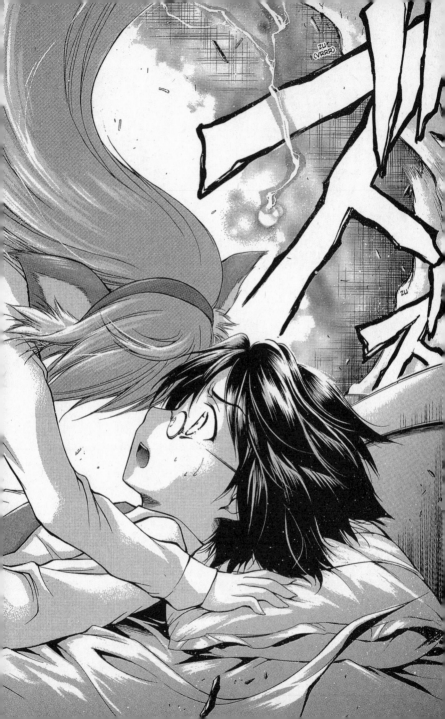

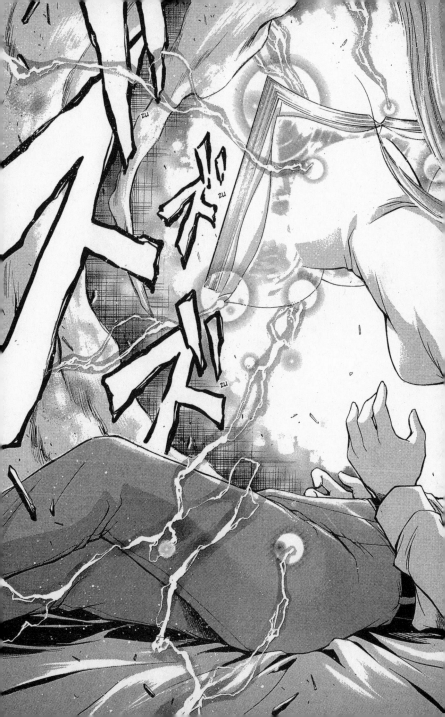

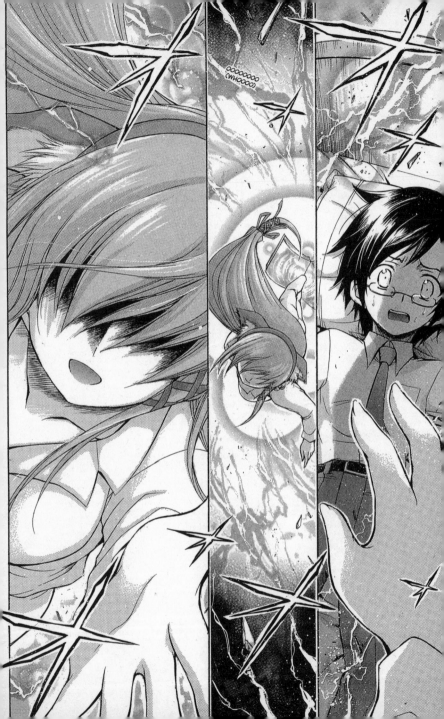

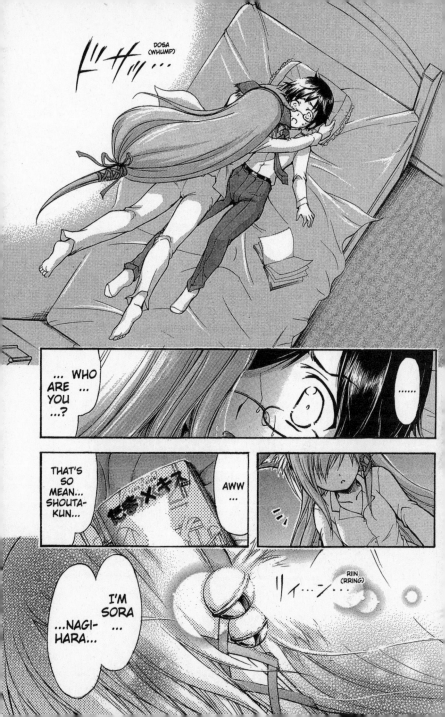

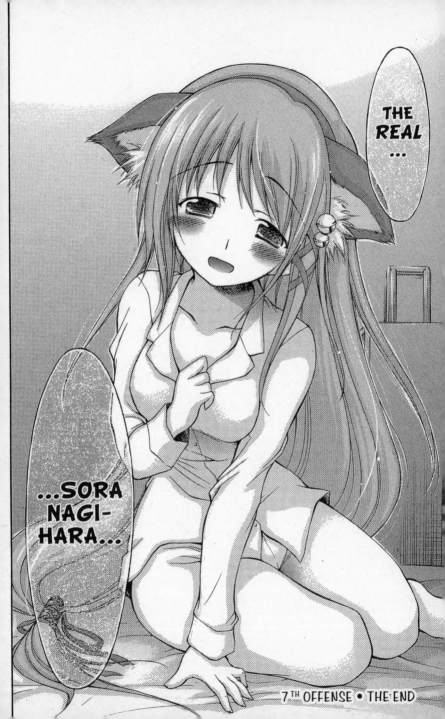

THIS WORK IS FICTION.
IT HAS NO RELATION TO ACTUAL
PEOPLES, ENTITIES, OR INCIDENTS.
ESPECIALLY NOT TO
MY MANGAKA SENPAI
LIVING IN FUKUOKA.
...OKAY?

SUU MINAZUKI

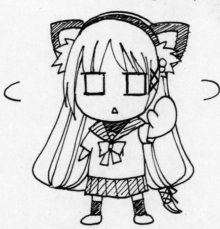

TWO

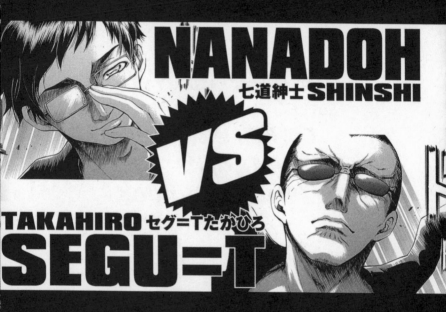

MIGHTY RIVALS

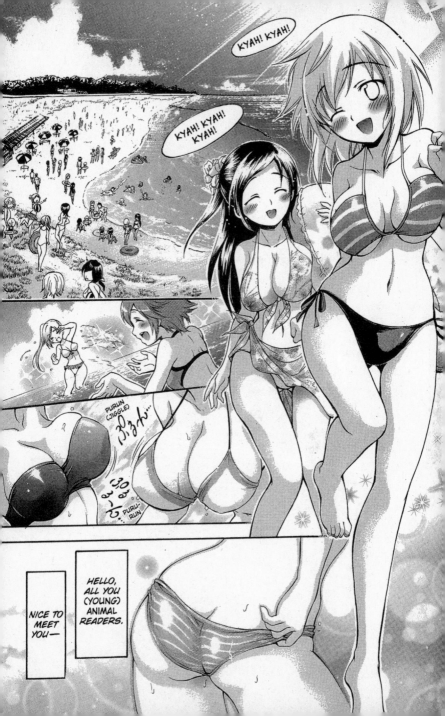

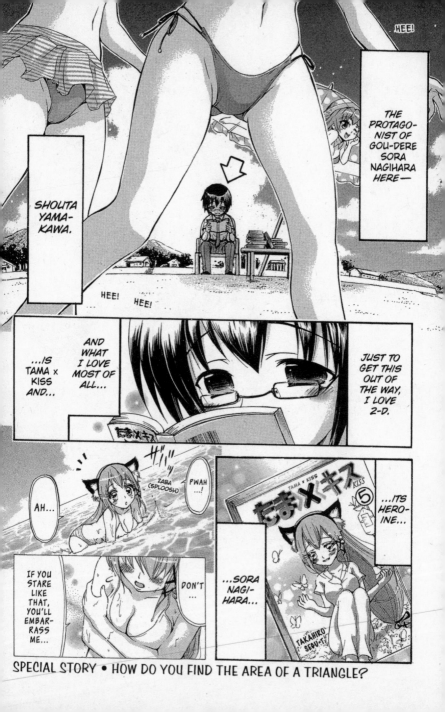

HEE!

THE PROTAGONIST OF GOU-DERE SORA NAGIHARA HERE—

SHOUTA YAMAKAWA.

HEE! HEE!

JUST TO GET THIS OUT OF THE WAY, I LOVE 2-D.

AND WHAT I LOVE MOST OF ALL...

...IS TAMA x KISS AND...

AH...

ZABA (SPLOOSH)

PWAH...!

IF YOU STARE LIKE THAT, YOU'LL EMBARRASS ME...

DON'T...

...SORA NAGIHARA...

...ITS HEROINE...

TAMA x KISS

TAMA x KISS

5

TAKAHIRO SEGU-T

SPECIAL STORY • HOW DO YOU FIND THE AREA OF A TRIANGLE?

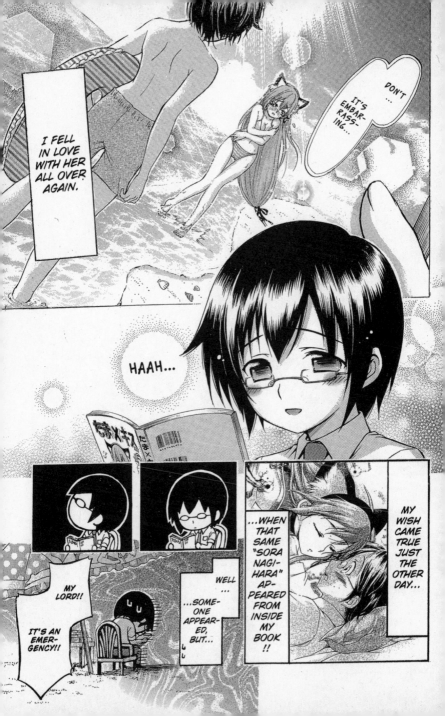

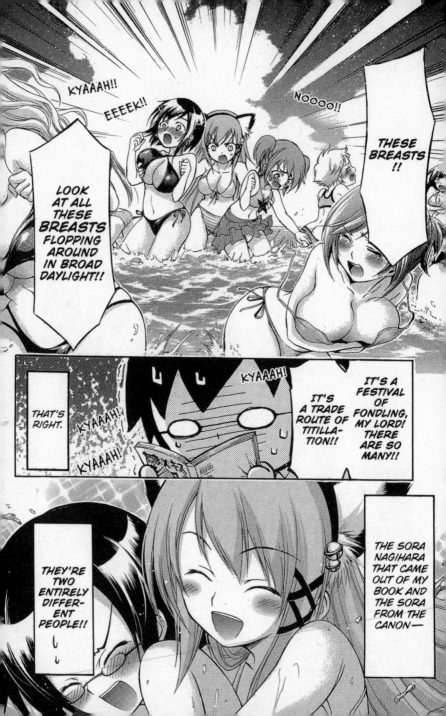

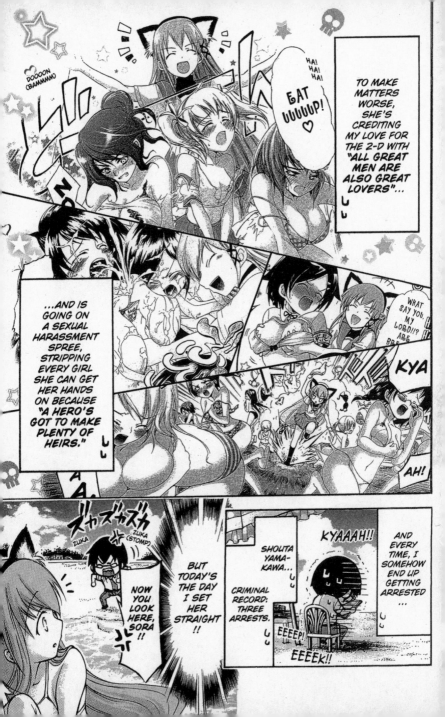

HAI HAI HAI!

EAT UUUUUP! ♡

TO MAKE MATTERS WORSE, SHE'S CREDITING MY LOVE FOR THE 2-D WITH "ALL GREAT MEN ARE ALSO GREAT LOVERS"...

DOOON (BAMMMM)

...AND IS GOING ON A SEXUAL HARASSMENT SPREE, STRIPPING EVERY GIRL SHE CAN GET HER HANDS ON BECAUSE "A HERO'S GOT TO MAKE PLENTY OF HEIRS."

WHAT SAY YOU, MY LORD!!?

KYA

AH!

ZUKA ZUKA ZUKA (STOMP)

NOW YOU LOOK HERE, SORA !!

BUT TODAY'S THE DAY I SET HER STRAIGHT !!

SHOUTA YAMA-KAWA...

CRIMINAL RECORD: THREE ARRESTS.

KYAAAAH!!

EEEEP!

EEEEEK!!

AND EVERY TIME, I SOMEHOW END UP GETTING ARRESTED ...

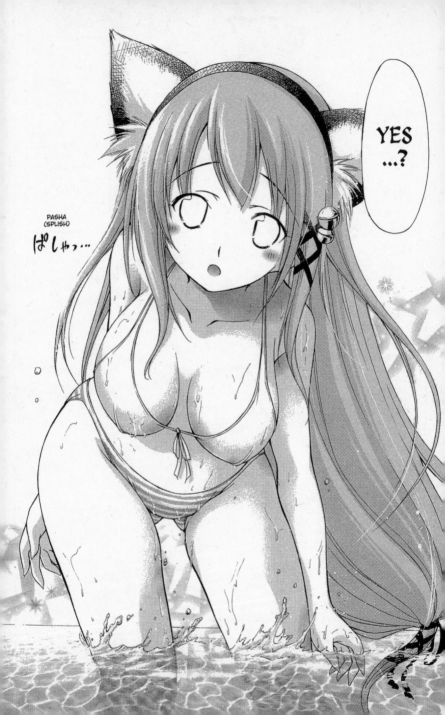

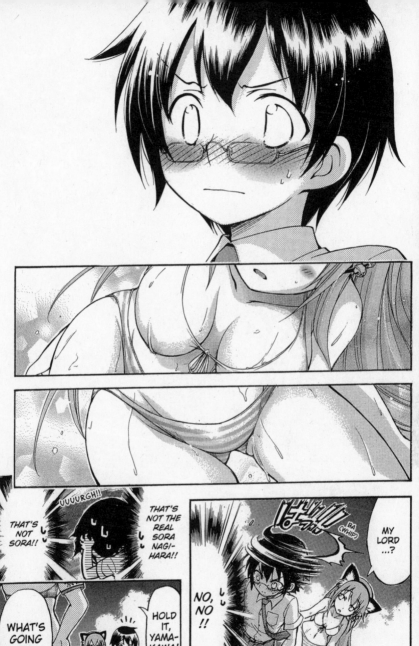

UUUURGH!!

THAT'S NOT SORA!!

THAT'S NOT THE REAL SORA NAGI-HARA!!

MY LORD ...?

BA (WHIP)

NO, NO !!

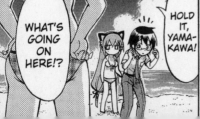

WHAT'S GOING ON HERE!?

HOLD IT, YAMA-KAWA!

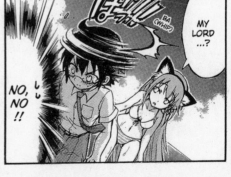

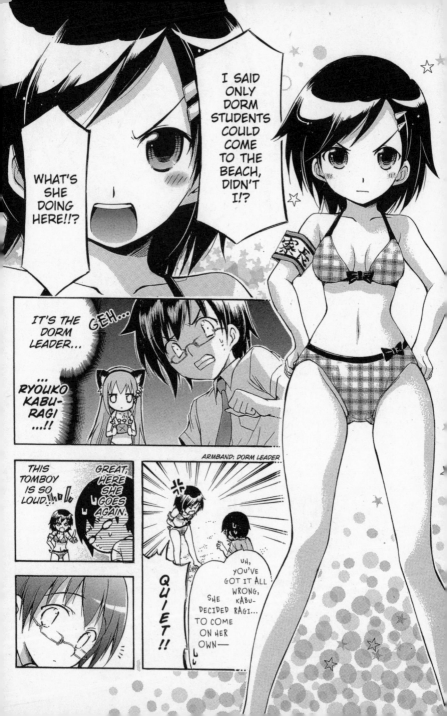

I SAID ONLY DORM STUDENTS COULD COME TO THE BEACH, DIDN'T I!?

WHAT'S SHE DOING HERE!!?

IT'S THE DORM LEADER...

GEH...

...RYŌUKO KABU-RAGI ...!!

ARMBAND: DORM LEADER

THIS TOMBOY IS SO LOUD.!!

GREAT, HERE SHE GOES AGAIN.

QUIET!!

UH, YOU'VE GOT IT ALL WRONG, KABU-RAGI... SHE DECIDED TO COME ON HER OWN—

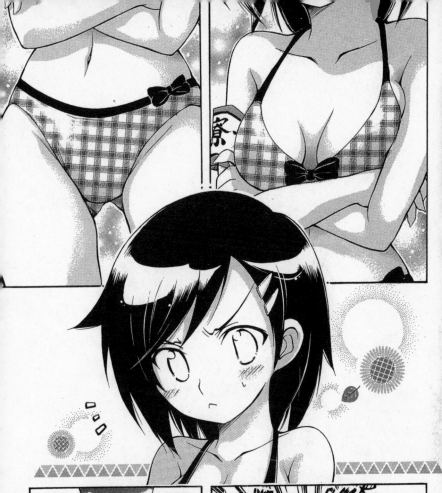

NOT LIKE I REALLY WANNA LOOK ANYWAY...

OKAY, OKAY, I GET IT. I WON'T LOOK. I WON'T LOOK...

BASHI (SMACK)

B F F F !!

AND JUST WHAT ARE YOU GAWKING AT!?

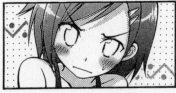

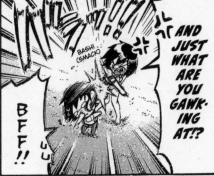

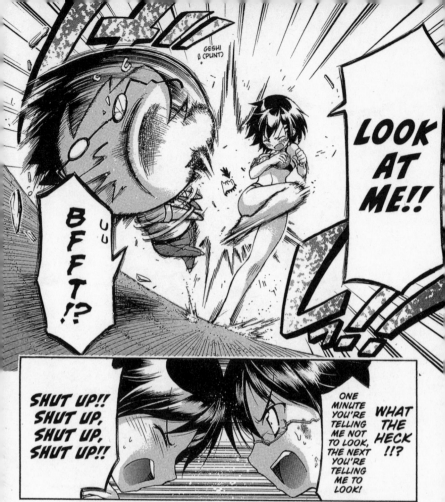

GESHI (PUNT)

LOOK AT ME!!

BFFT!!?

SHUT UP!! SHUT UP, SHUT UP, SHUT UP!!

ONE MINUTE YOU'RE TELLING ME NOT TO LOOK, THE NEXT YOU'RE TELLING ME TO LOOK!

WHAT THE HECK!!?

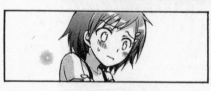

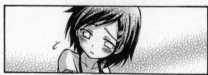

CAN I LOOK!? OR NOT!?

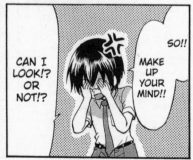

SO!! MAKE UP YOUR MIND!!

180

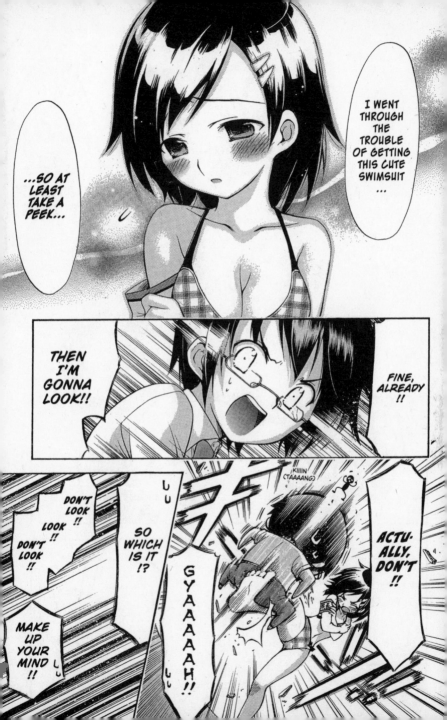

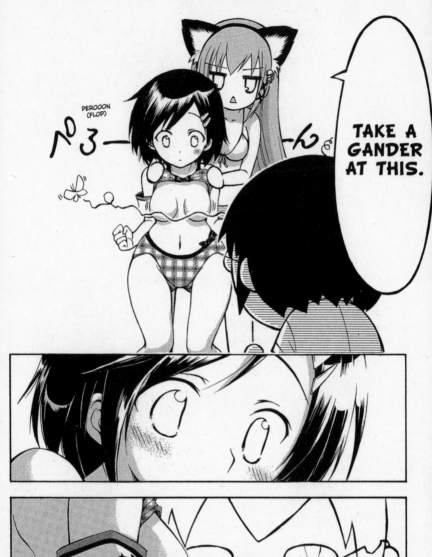

PEROOON
(FLOP)

TAKE A
GANDER
AT THIS.

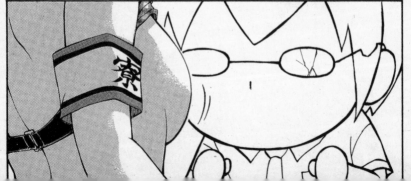

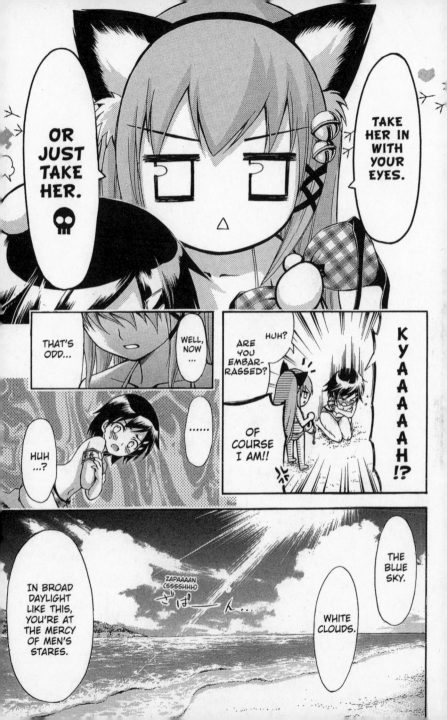

OR JUST TAKE HER. ☠

TAKE HER IN WITH YOUR EYES.

THAT'S ODD...

WELL, NOW...

HUH...?

......

ARE YOU EMBAR- RASSED?

HUH?

OF COURSE I AM!!

KYAAAAAH!?

IN BROAD DAYLIGHT LIKE THIS, YOU'RE AT THE MERCY OF MEN'S STARES.

THE BLUE SKY.

WHITE CLOUDS.

ZAPAAAAN (SSSSHHH)

AND
EVERY-
BODY...

...IS
RUNNING
AROUND
HALF-
NAKED
...!?

BABAN
(BABAM)

WELL,
WE'RE
AT THE
BEACH—

UH...
BUT
SEE,
THIS
IS...

THEY'RE
SOAKED
RIGHT
THROUGH
!!

AND
THEY'RE
GOING
RIGHT INTO
THE OCEAN
TO GET
DRIPPING
WET!!

HUH
...
BATHING
SUITS
...?

WE'RE ALL
WEARING
BATHING
SUITS, SO
THERE'S
NOTHING TO
BE EMBAR-
RASSED
ABOUT!

ARE
YOU
SOME
KIND OF
IDIOT!?

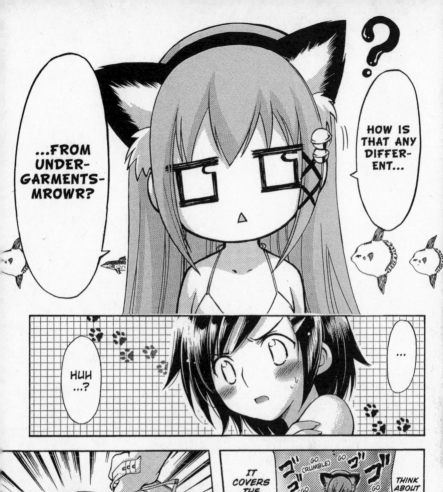

...FROM UNDER-GARMENTS-MROWR?

HOW IS THAT ANY DIFFER-ENT...

HUH ...?

...

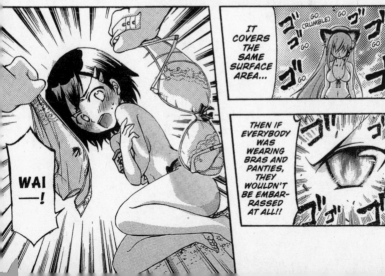

IT COVERS THE SAME SURFACE AREA...

THINK ABOUT IT...

GO (RUMBLE)

THEN IF EVERYBODY WAS WEARING BRAS AND PANTIES, THEY WOULDN'T BE EMBAR-RASSED AT ALL!!

A-HA, THAT'S IT!!

WAI—!

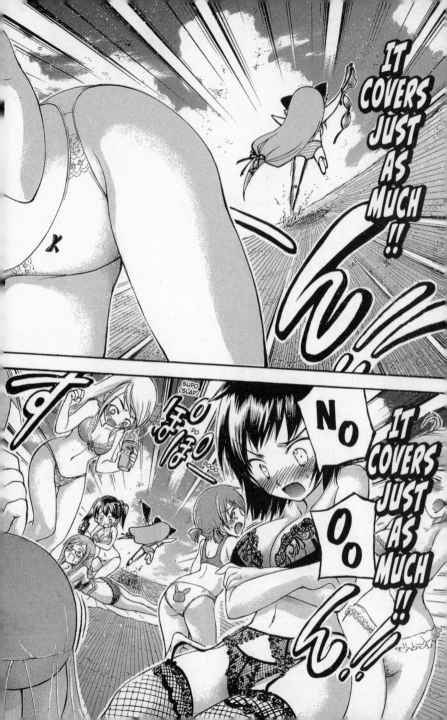

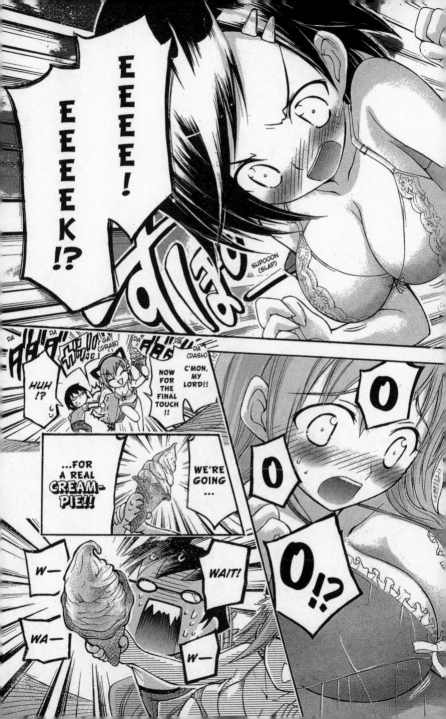

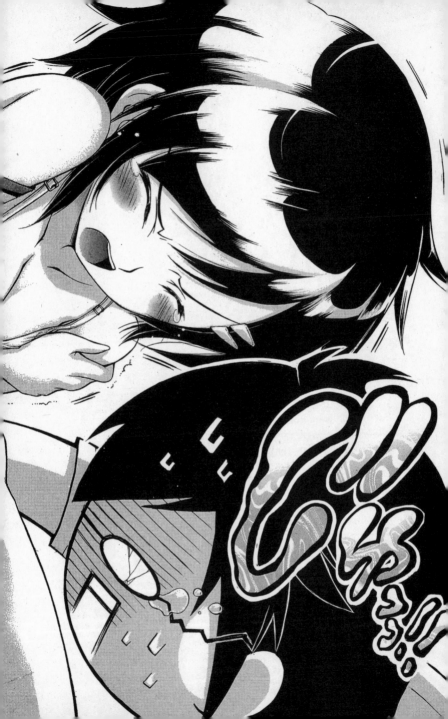

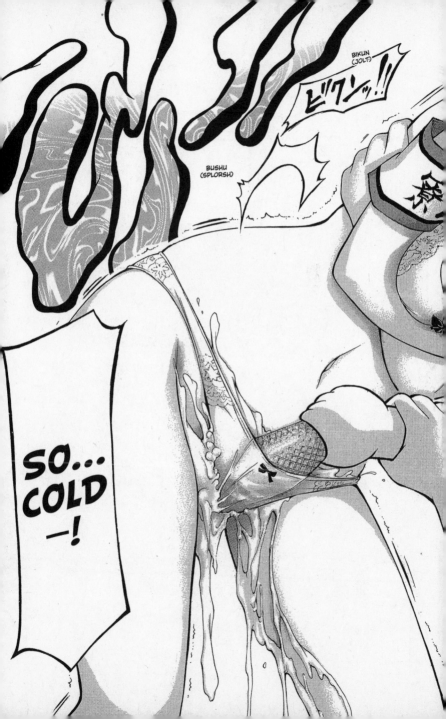

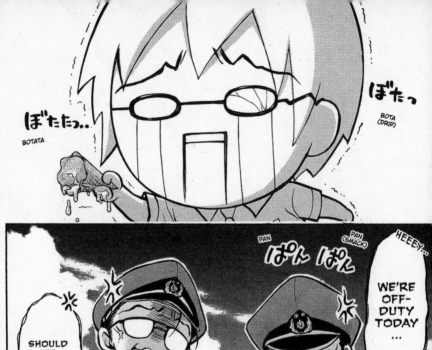

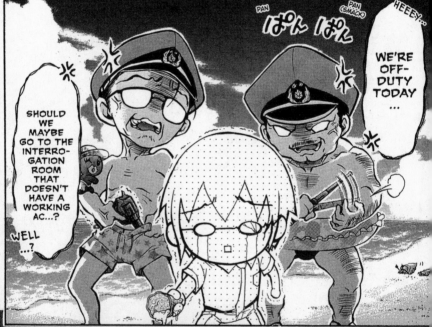

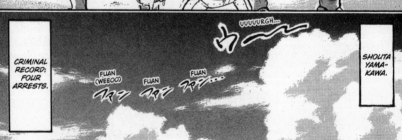

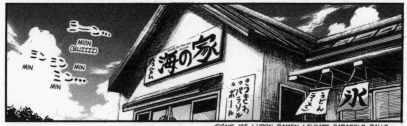

SIGNS: ICE / UDON, RAMEN / FLOATS, PARASOLS, BALLS

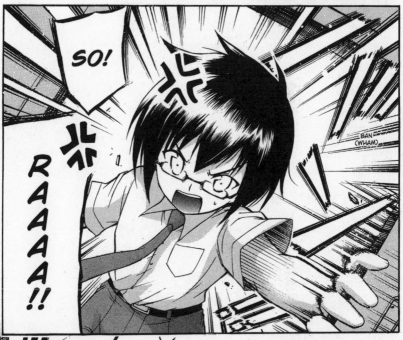

SO!

RAAAA!!

BAN (WHAM)

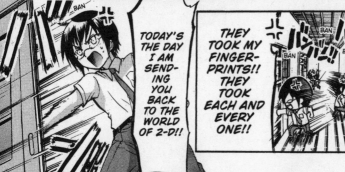

TODAY'S THE DAY I AM SENDING YOU BACK TO THE WORLD OF 2-D!!

THEY TOOK MY FINGER-PRINTS!! THEY TOOK EACH AND EVERY ONE!!

WHERE ARE YOU!!? WHERE ARE YOU HIDING —!?

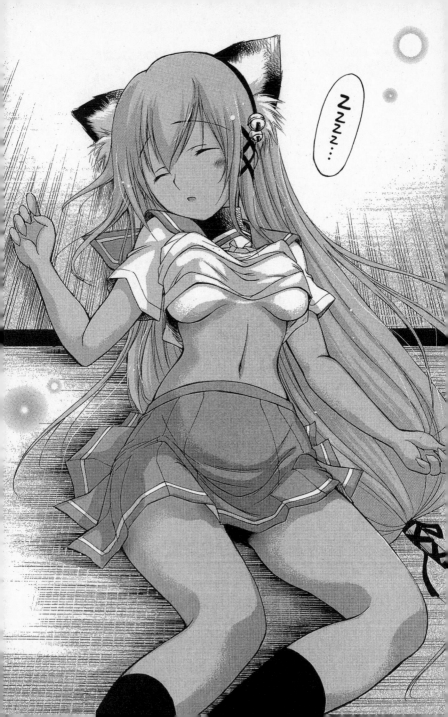

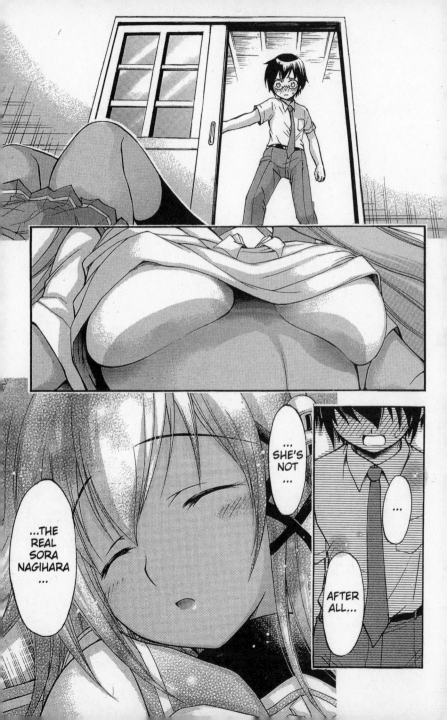

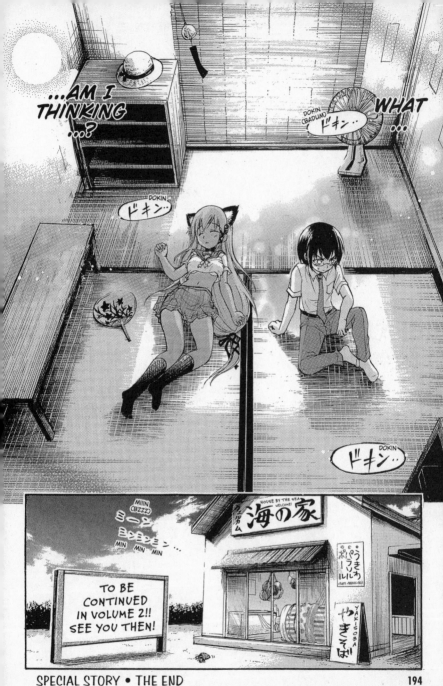

SPECIAL STORY • THE END

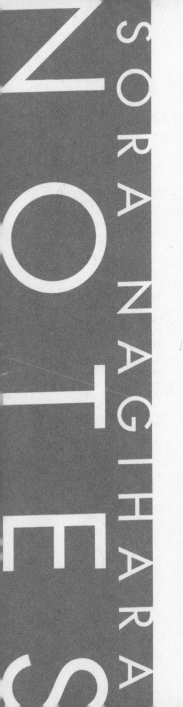

PAGE 2
The kanji on the curtains behind Sora read "men's bath."

PAGE 30
Dorm leader **Ryouko Kaburagi**'s name is a bit of a pun, since the word for dorm in Japanese is *ryou*.

PAGE 45
Animo in Animo Academy means "Fight!" or "Come on!" in Spanish.

PAGE 46-47
The names of the Moro'oka sisters have related meanings. **Tenka** is spelled with the kanji for "heavenly flower," while **Chika** uses the characters for "earthly flower."

PAGE 57
Absolute territory, or *zettai ryouiki*, refers to a girl's exposed skin between the top of socks or stockings and the hemline of her skirt. The term is thought to be a nod to the classic anime *Neon Genesis Evangelion*.

PAGE 93
Devil, come this way/toward the clapping hands are the opening lyrics to the song "[KR] Cube" by Japanese metal band DIR EN GREY.

PAGE 151
Makiko is a minor character from another Suu Minazuki manga, *Heaven's Lost Property* (*Sora no Otoshimono*).

PAGE 171
Young Animal is the Japanese manga magazine anthology in which *Gou-Dere* is serialized.

GOU-DERE
SORA NAGIHARA ❶

SUU MINAZUKI

Translation: Christine Dashiell • Lettering: James Dashiell

Gou-Dere Bishojo Nagihara Sora by Suu Minazuki
© Suu Minazuki 2011
All rights reserved.
First published in Japan in 2011 by HAKUSENSHA, INC., Tokyo. English language translation rights in U.S.A., Canada and U.K. arranged with HAKUSENSHA, INC., Tokyo through Tuttle-Mori Agency Inc., Tokyo.

Translation © 2014 Hachette Book Group, Inc.

Yen Press
Hachette Book Group
1290 Avenue of the Americas
New York, NY 10104

www.HachetteBookGroup.com
www.YenPress.com

Yen Press is an imprint of Hachette Book Group, Inc. The Yen Press name and logo are trademarks of Hachette Book Group, Inc.

First Yen Press Edition: November 2014

ISBN: 978-0-316-33663-5

10 9 8 7 6 5 4 3 2

BVG

Printed in the United States of America